Five l Laugh

Julian G. Martin (signature)

if x/y=z
23/3=1/8 **then**
40/20=1/2 x>y
60/40=2/3

When my daughter Debbie was three,
She was one-eighth my age twenty-three.
By twenty she was half
forty—two-thirds—such math,
And now she is older than me!

Julian G. Martin

EAKIN PRESS ✦ Austin, Texas

FIRST EDITION
Copyright © 2000
By Julian G. Martin

Published in the United States of America
By Eakin Press
A Division of Sunbelt Media, Inc.
P.O. Drawer 90159 ☐ Austin, Texas 78709-0159
email: eakinpub@sig.net
☐ website: www.eakinpress.com ☐
ALL RIGHTS RESERVED.

1 2 3 4 5 6 7 8 9

1-57168-495-6

For CIP information, please access:
www.loc.gov

Designed and Illustrated by Liz Martin.
Text was set in Franklin Gothic Book typeface.
Limericks were set in Franklin Gothic Demi.
Subheadings were set in Goudy Heavyface, and
chapter titles were set in American Uncial.

Five Lines & a Laugh

Table of Contents

foreword & acknowledgments

A review of the five-line limerick throughout its 150-plus years of history reveals a limited purpose that cries for expansion. Much of the earlier literature was devoted to nonsensical rhymes that appealed to young children in a nursery setting. As the modern limerick pattern of five lines evolved during the twentieth century, those favoring its use as a ribald form of entertainment for adults won out over those favoring alternate uses. "Clean" limericks, for example, were summarily dismissed. Only a "dirty" limerick could be a good limerick.

My assessment of the limerick as an instrument of expression allows for a much broader purpose. While nonsensical and earthy limericks deserve a place at the table, the limerick is too good an instrument to be restricted to those categories. I say let it be used to brighten one's day in ever so many ways.

This book explores several possibilities. Limericks can be used for voice mail greetings, family celebrations of all kinds, class reunions, advocacy of a cause, and family histories, to name a few. Why not make the limerick a lighthearted, useful art form, giving it a touch of class that transcends barroom humor? Such a question may stir yet another round of conflict among limerick lovers as opposing sides once again gird for battle over the proper use of limericks.

I say let the debate begin:

A limerick I put to good use
Is like trumping an ace with a deuce,
Or Dave o'er Goliath,
Or love that satisfyeth,
Or finding one's tooth is not loose.

In other words, it feels real good!

Since that is true, what better way to acknowledge my appreciation to many of those who helped me "place this project in print" than to place them in a series of limericks and four-liners.

First were the established authors, who were kind enough to review my book and offer advice and encouragement needed to make this book a reality. It is a great feeling to have friends in high places.

Historian Goodwyn, whose first name is Larry,
Gave a thrust that wiped out my parry;
"Know your audience," said he,
"Or your message will flee."
So I lined up with Tom, Dick, and Harry!

Dr. Goodwyn is a nationally known author. I had the pleasure of working with him in a resource role for his book entitled "Texas Oil, American Dreams" a few years ago. He helped me define the "thrust" of my limerick treatise and to whom it might appeal.

Equally helpful was the late Texas icon Jack Maguire, whose many accomplishments included a book entitled *A Treasury of Texas Tales*, which is being published this year.

Jack Maguire knew Texas lore,
From sipping tea to saddle sore.
He took one look
And read my book.
"Publish," he cried, "it's laughs galore!"

Valuable editing and encouragement came from theologian author George Ricker and mystery writer Nancy Bell.

> **A stickler was my editor George Ricker;**
> **With him I couldn't bicker or dicker.**
> **His thirst for perfection**
> **Caused multiple correction.**
> **No wonder he once served as my vicar!**

> **My daughter's namesake, Nancy Bell,**
> **Writes books that actually sell.**
> **So I found it real neat**
> **And leaped to my feet,**
> **When she urged that I publish pell-mell!**

Two more authors, Dr. Margaret Berry, who has tracked the colorful history of the University of Texas in print, and Willie Kocurek, who wrote his life story as a one of a kind legendary Texan from Dime Box, a quiet Central Texas community, would not let me say, "No, I can't end up in print." Thank heaven, they and others prevailed.

> **Margaret Berry, historian for U.T.**
> **And Texas legend Kocurek, Willeee**
> **Helped make my day**
> **By pointing the way**
> **From a book dream to reality.**

Family support was vital to this project, and it was there from the beginning to the end. Those members who helped are in the following four-liners.

> **A special thanks to my own family,**
> **Wife Lois, daughters Debbie and Nancy;**
> **Add sons-in-law Robert and Terry,**
> **Finally a hug for granddaughter Dawn E.**

> **To brother Steve, wife Lisa, and daughter Stephanie;**
> **Son Peter and Elizabeth who drew pics for me,**
> **I express appreciation for their shouts of glee;**
> **It made me want-to-publish for all the world to see.***

*If you believe that, I have several copies for sale ...

Others who became involved, read manuscripts, and offered helpful hints included college chums Jo and Deke Lang and Peggy Estill, and fellow duplicate bridge player Patty Pels. Second-milers who provided invaluable administrative and public relations assistance included Sandra Bloodworth, Gloria Hooper, and Lucianna McKeown.

The Division of Continuing & Extended Education at the University of Texas at Austin, under the direction of Dr. Tom Hatfield, gave me numerous opportunities to conduct seminars on material in my book. These included appearances before SAGE (Seminars for Adult Growth and Enrichment), LAMP (Learning Activities for Mature People) and the UT Elderhostel program, headed by Nancy Seelig. These experiences provided an excellent testing ground for final editing purposes.

❧ chapter one :
Background

The only good limerick is a simple, nonsensical, and absurd limerick that is obscene in nature. If you believe that and are too obstinate to change your mind on anything, you have no business reading this book. If, on the other hand, you profess to have an open mind on the subject, be prepared to pursue the following proposition (sorry about the alliteration, but we need to get in the mood early here). A good limerick can be clever, well made, witty, funny, clean, and useful—all at the same time!

"In your face," you say. "I have yet to read one that has all those can be's." Actually, it will be best if you haven't, for this will allow me to fill a corner of that open mind of yours with fresh material for you to enjoy or use. Yes, the key word is *use*. In Chapters Two through Six, original material is presented to illustrate how limericks and four-liners can serve to lighten one's day, whether it be voice mail, a family celebration, or a reunion of some kind. If you develop the ability to write limericks, you can have a lot of fun using them for all sorts of special occasions.

Before we get into the good stuff, we should spend a little time reviewing the history of the limerick and how it was technically developed into the instrument it is today. Keep in mind that this is neither a history book nor a training manual. Yet, you need to know what it takes to write a good, useful limerick, for some of you may find the urge to write one by the end of this book (to the absolute delight of your former friends).

No one knows who wrote the first limerick or when he or she did so. There are poems in literature predating Shakespeare that give a hint of the limerick form to come, but it was not until the early 1800s that the poem form began to take hold. Apparently named after the town of Limerick in Ireland, the earliest limericks were obviously designed to amuse children. A classic example of this is the nursery rhyme entitled, "Hickory, Dickory Dock."

One of the earliest authors to lay the predicate for modern limericks was Edward Lear, whose *Book of Nonsense* was published in 1846, again to amuse children. Unfortunately, his prodigious collection bordered on the boring for adults, aggravated, perhaps, by his virtually repeating the first line of the limerick in the fifth and last line. As we shall see, the fifth line is absolutely essential to the development of a good limerick and should not be wasted through meaningless repetition. Since Lear specialized in clean limericks, his work may have fed the ongoing claim by George Bernard Shaw and others during the ensuing 150 years that only ribald limericks are fit to print—an argument that is carried on to this day.

Lear, however, should not be lightly dismissed. Unless someone else surfaces, he should receive credit for perfecting the modern five-line limerick form. Many of his limericks were technically sound, even though they dealt in nonsense to appeal to young readers. Let's look at some examples of his work to get the picture. First, a couple of limericks that are really difficult to appreciate from an adult's point of view:

> **There was an Old Person of Prague,**
> **Who was suddenly seized with the plague;**
> **But they gave him some butter,**
> **Which caused him to mutter,**
> **And cured that Old Person of Prague.**

Can you spot the problems? Prague does not rhyme with plague, despite the spelling. Even with the acceptable nonsense theme, it is a bit of a stretch to claim butter causes muttering. Finally, the last line's zing—which we discuss later—is diluted by the repetitious phrasing. Another example:

> **There was an Old Man of Corfu,**
> **Who never knew what he should do:**
>> **So he rushed up and down,**
>> **Till the sun made him brown,**
> **That bewildered Old Man of Corfu.**

Whether this limerick was as successful as "Hickory, Hickory Dock" in conjuring up humorous images for children is not known, but it does little for the adult mind.

Some of Lear's limericks came closer to amusing adults. If he had dedicated the fifth line as a punch line for this purpose he would perhaps have amused them as he did children with his more innocent works. For example:

> **There was an Old Man of Coblenz,**
> **The length of whose legs was immense;**
>> **He went with one prance,**
>> **From Turkey to France,**
> **That surprising Old Man of Coblenz.**

Now see what happens when the fifth line is rewritten to provide an adult punch.

> **There was an Old Man of Coblenz,**
> **The length of whose legs was immense;**
>> **He went with one prance,**
>> **From Turkey to France,**
> **But straddled the Alps with pain quite intense!**

Lost innocence is the result! Another example:

> **There was an old man of West Dumpet,**
> **Who possessed a large nose like a trumpet;**
>> **When he blew it aloud,**
>> **It astonished the crowd,**
> **And was heard through the whole of West Dumpet.**

Undoubtedly, children enjoy the imagery this fine limerick provides them, but adults are hung up over an interfering mystery; namely, what "crowd?" Why not put the vital fifth line to good use to provide the answer? Like so:

> **There was an old man of West Dumpet,**
> **Who possessed a large nose like a trumpet;**
> **When he blew it aloud,**
> **It astonished the crowd,**
> **That was throwing small stones at a strumpet.**

This change does not a classic make nor does stoning of a strumpet lend itself to humor, but at least the story is now complete, with a touch of desirable alliteration to help spruce things up.

Returning to the original debate of what makes a limerick worth listening to, the author has dabbled in both the clean and the ribald for years and has come to this conclusion: Whether a limerick is good or not has virtually nothing to do with its cleanliness or lack of it. A good limerick is one that tells a clever story, is technically correct or close to it, is rich in rhyme, is humorous or ironic, and has a fifth line that provides fabulous closure. To this list add useful purpose, without which this book would not be written.

While reading numerous books on limericks in preparation for this treatise, I have noted that many of the better limericks through the years were written by authors unknown and have been inserted again and again into the collections modern writers present to their readers. In this first chapter, there is a relative handful of these to illustrate the various features that make up a good limerick. In the process of reviewing these classics, pay close attention to the techniques involved in modern limerick writing so that you, the reader, may try your hand in writing your own. Consider yourself warned, however (as you will be again in Chapter Five), that the writing of a mere five-line limerick is not as easy as it appears. As we shall see, even reading one or presenting one orally can be a challenge. However, you will find the effort worthwhile, for limericks can be a lot of fun.

A limerick is always a five-line composition. The first, second, and fifth lines are the longer lines, which end with words that rhyme. The third and fourth lines are shorter and also end with words that rhyme. A good limerick must flow like a well-written piece of music in order to be successful. Although there are tricks we shall mention later that help preserve a good limerick by fudging on the flow, a decent flow is absolutely essential.

To secure the flow, the limerick writer must pay attention to a few basic rules. He (she) must first establish a good, consistent rhythm (or meter) throughout the limerick. What this really means is choosing words with the right number of syllables, as well as accented syllables appropriately located to make each of the five lines flow when they are read or presented orally.

This can be illustrated by providing a "la" for each syllable in an appropriately metered limerick, underlining the "la's" that must be emphasized (or accented) to make the limerick flow:

> **La <u>la</u>, la la <u>la</u>, la la <u>la</u>,**
> **La <u>la</u>, la la <u>la</u>, la la <u>la</u>,**
> **La <u>la</u>, la la <u>la</u>,**
> **La <u>la</u>, la la <u>la</u>,**
> **La <u>la</u>, la la <u>la</u>, la la <u>la</u>.**

As mentioned earlier, there are written and oral mechanisms that allow us to abuse slightly this rather strict rhythmic pattern. But for now, you as the aspiring limerick writer must keep this basic pattern in mind. You might practice by citing the "la's" a few times to get the "feel of the flow" (sorry!).

Let's mess with an old limerick to show why these structure rules are essential and how they apply. Suppose the first line read:

There **WAS** \ a bear **THAT** \ was old **AND** \ was cheer**FUL** \ while liv**ING** \ at the **CIT** \ y zoo;

Hopefully, it should be obvious to all who scan this line that this limerick attempt will not flow into success. Aside from the horrendous license taken in constructing a sentence, the line is more than twice as long as the normal limerick first line is. Furthermore, the accented syllables, with the possible exception of the first one, emphasize procedural words or syllables that do not lend themselves to a cogent story. As written, the limerick line does not flow. Now, see what happens when we read the first line as originally written:

A **CHEER** \ ful old **BEAR** \ at the **ZOO**;

Note that the line provides the same information that the first attempt did. But it is in harness with the rules and, therefore, flows in its simple clarity. For those of you who have not read or heard this old-timer before, here it is in its full and original glory:

> **A cheerful old bear at the zoo**
> **Could always find something to do.**
>   **When it bored him, you know**
>   **To walk to and fro,**
> **He reversed it and walked fro and to.**

This is a fine old limerick that has withstood the test of time. Surely, however, you are discerning enough to note that it does not strictly follow the rules. For example, the third line has an extra "la" in it! Instead of La **la**, la la **la**, it reads la la **la**, la la **la**. Horrors! This can be overcome by reading or citing the third line so that the phrase "When it" runs together and therefore sounds like the one syllable allowed under the rules. A similar problem exists in the fifth line, where the reader must treat the word "reversed" as though it had one syllable. Remember the earlier comment that a good limerick need not be sacrificed by strict adherence to the rules, as long as the diversion is minor and not disruptive.

There are a few more don'ts to explore before you leave the exercise room and begin play on the court. We have just explored how a good limerick follows a *la **la**, la la **la**, la la **la*** meter pattern, such as:

There **ONCE** was a **MAN** who was **FUNNY**;

Once you have mastered this vital fundamental, do not fall into the trap many aspiring limercists (if that has not been a word, it is now!) do by thinking that this syllabic emphasis in reverse, namely, ***la** la la, **la** la la, **la** la*, is also good limerick construction, such as:

                                  ඐ ᒍulian g. martin

TENDerly, **TEND**erly, **JE**sus is **CALL**ing;

This may get you into your church choir, if you are a Christian, but it definitely will not get you into the limerick writers' hall of fame. Actually, it may not get you into the choir, either, because the line should read, "Softly and tenderly Jesus is calling ...!"

Okay. It is time to lighten up a little with some classical limericks that illustrate what can be done to make a limerick unique or outstanding. Unfortunately, these limericks are by authors unknown, to me at least, which illustrates the general disease afflicting limerick history— limerick writers are usually too modest or too interested in their own welfare to admit to such authorship! So let's move on in our ignorance and begin with a limerick that has almost perfect meter throughout its text:

> **There was an old man of Blackheath,**
> **Who sat on his set of false teeth.**
> **Said he, with a start,**
> **"O Lord, bless my heart!**
> **I've bitten myself underneath!"**

When the meter rhythm is this good, the limerick is easily read in public, for the need for oral inflection is reduced.

There are several good features in the next limerick. First, it is a rare example of legitimate usage of the same rhyming word at the end of the first and last lines. This is acceptable here, because the word has an entirely different meaning in the two lines. Also, there is an internal rhyme in the fifth line that adds punch to the limerick, despite the fact that both of the rhyming words are used elsewhere in the limerick. Very unusual. Finally, the limerick provides a classic example of a vital fifth line carrying the day and giving closure to a sad but humorous story.

> **There was an old man of Nantucket,**
> **Who kept all his cash in a bucket;**
> **But his daughter named Nan**
> **Ran away with a man,**
> **And as for the bucket—Nantucket!**

The following limerick also has a unique fifth line, thanks to the clever use of a well-known saying:

> **A maiden at college, named Breeze,**
> **Weighed down by B.A.s and M.D.s,**
> **Collapsed from the strain.**
> **Said her doctor, " 'Tis plain**
> **You are killing yourself—by degrees."**

Yet another example of a superb last line, dealing not only in tragic absurdity, but also jerking the reader or listener about in a new and startling direction, concludes the following limerick:

> **There once was a girl named O'Brien**
> **Who taught holy hymns to a lion;**
> **Of the lady there's some**
> **In the lion's tum-tum;**
> **The rest twangs a harp up in Zion.**

Next, a final illustration on outstanding fifth lines. The following oldie has a great last line, not because of substance, but because of a fantastic internal rhyme:

> **The bottle of perfume that Willie sent**
> **Was highly displeasing to Millicent.**
> **Her thanks were so cold,**
> **They quarreled, I'm told,**
> **O'er that silly scent Willie sent Millicent.**

As you can see, the actual message of the fifth line is quite ordinary, but the way it is expressed is exquisite indeed. Many of the classical limericks depend on alliteration—the use of many words starting with the same letter—to achieve cleverness. Some are much better than others, as is the following:

> **A fly and a flea in a flue**
> **Were imprisoned, so what could they do?**
> **Said the fly, "Let us flee!"**
> **"Let us fly," said the flea.**
> **So they flew through a flaw in the flue.**

Next we have two excellent limericks that tell a story based on con-
ceivable fact rather than fantasy. They help prove that a good limerick does not have to be groundless, silly, or ribald to be good. Here
they are:

> **There was a young fellow of Perth,**
> **Who was born on the day of his birth.**
> > **He was married, they say,**
> > **On his wife's wedding day,**
> **And he died—when he quitted the earth.**

> **A rocket explorer named Wright**
> **Once traveled much faster than light.**
> > **He set out one day**
> > **In a relative way,**
> **And returned on the previous night.**

Lest you think the latter limerick is fantasy and not fact, you have not
read Einstein or crossed the international date line in a Concorde!

On the other hand, do not assume that a fanciful limerick cannot also
be a lot of fun and just as clever. Witness the following!

> **There was a fool gardener of Leeds,**
> **Rashly swallowed six packets of seeds.**
> > **In a month, silly ass,**
> > **He was covered with grass,**
> **And he couldn't sit down for the weeds.**

> **They hanged an old lady in Baltimore**
> **Who mentioned two things they should alter more.**
> > **"This noose, now," she said,**
> > **"Won't go over my head,**
> **And I wish they would lengthen the halter more."**

Note that both of these outstanding limericks disobey the basic rule
applying to the number of syllables recommended for the five lines.
Again, in the case of limericks, rules are meant to be broken as long
as the result justifies variation. This is the case here. Although all lines

have excessive syllables, the excess is consistent, allowing the lines to read well. Furthermore, the subject matter is excellent, which is a must when poetic license is taken.

Still other limericks depend solely on the pun, an embarrassing predicament, or a point of view to attract attention. First, the pun:

> **There was a young girl, a sweet lamb,**
> **Who smiled as she entered a tram.**
> > **After she had embarked,**
> > **The conductor remarked,**
> **"Your fare." And she said, "Yes, I am."**

The embarrassing predicament:

> **There was a queer lady named Harris,**
> **Whom nothing could ever embarrass**
> > **Till the bath salts she shook**
> > **In the bath that she took**
> **Turned out to be plaster of Paris.**

And the propa ... ah, excuse me, point of view:

> **A Tory, once out in his motor,**
> **Ran over a Laborite voter.**
> > **"Thank goodness," he cried,**
> > **"He was on the wrong side,**
> **So I don't blame myself one iota."**

For those unfamiliar with British rules of the road, drivers in England drive on the left side of the road, while most of the world drives on the right. This bit of information is necessary to enjoy the double meaning hidden in this classic.

Now, as you prepare to move on to the useful use of limericks, four-liner poems, and true short stories, we close the first chapter with a limerick gem that will help you keep in mind the utmost importance of the meter in creating the proper rhythmic flow for our limericks. Here it is:

A decrepit old gas man named Peter,
While hunting around for the meter,
Touched a leak with his light;
He arose out of sight,
And (as anyone can see by reading this),
it also destroyed the meter.

Isn't that beautiful?

cs chapter two:
phone voice mail greetings

Most people have voice mail gizmos attached to their phones that allow the caller to leave a message when they are not home to answer the phone. Now, there is nothing wrong with that, for it does tend to improve communication. But why make the caller suffer through a boring or misleading statement of greeting just for the privilege of leaving you a message that you may badly need? Surely, you have heard the following statements of greeting—or similar versions— through the years, but have you ever left a message that truly responds to these oral gems?

> **"You have reached 469-2371.**
> **Please leave your message at the tone ..."**
> "Hi, 469-2371. May I call you by your first name, 469? My name is 365-9334, '365' for short, and I'm having your baby on 9-I-97 in Room 1055 at 7:30 am in Ranch 6666 Hospital. Please call 455-0683, 243-5339, and 781-2099 to let them know. Thanks, 469, for your understanding and close personal touch."

> **"Hi; I can't get to the phone right now, but please leave your name and phone number, and I will return your call as soon as possible."**

"Hey, Joe. Your ASAP stinks. I happen to know you left for Greece this morning and won't be home for six weeks."

"At the sound of the tone, please leave your name, your address, your phone number(s), your ID, your social security number, the time you called, the reason you called, whether you know us personally or not, and we'll get back to you as soon as we have checked your political affiliation, called the sheriff, and interrogated IRS."
"I <u>was</u> your babysitter for tonight."

"This is__(blank)__Smith _____
ah, resi ____ (static) _____ is____ (blank) _____ .
Beep-beep-beep-beep-beep-beep-b e e e e e e e e e e e
e e e e e e e p.
"Perhaps your children will buy you a new machine for your birthday."

"We're not at home right now, so you'll just have to call us later."
"What on earth makes you think so?"

You and I both know we will never sound off with responses like that, but since we tend to feel that way at times, such recorded phone messages occasionally generate an undesirable background for our actual response. What can we do, then, to soften the blow of our absence when the caller calls?

My answer to this is a touch of humor through the use of limericks or four-liner Burma Shave-type poems. If you do this, however, there are a few basic guidelines to consider. First, be sure to change the message at least four times a year to give your frequent callers a break. Keep a record of them so that after four years or so, you can begin repeating your work. This is valid, because people tend to forget your literary gems, and many of us can't keep the same friends longer than four years anyway.

Next, while you can be a little salty and insulting at times to bolster your humor, do not poke fun at age, infirmity, or relatives. This can backfire when a friend or relative calls to announce that Aunt Susie is no longer with us or that nephew Ted has been diagnosed with a terminal illness.

Finally, steer clear of anything that will wind up with you in court or listening to this irate caller response: "You really don't get it, do you?" Humorous phone messages are not a forum for Archie Bunker philosophy, or the other end of the political spectrum, for that matter. The use of limericks in pursuit of a cause has its place elsewhere, as we shall see in a later chapter.

During the past decade, I have written fifty or so limericks and four-liners for use on the family phone. These do not include the losers that our "adoring phone public" helped us discard at an early age, which brings to mind the debate concerning clean versus dirty limericks discussed in Chapter One. As you may well imagine, dirty limericks really have no acceptable role in phone answering messages. For example, you never know when your preacher may call! At the same time, this complicates the task of writing acceptable poems, for the writer must keep in mind the thought expressed in the following limerick by an author unknown:

> **The limerick packs laughs anatomical**
> **Into space that is quite economical.**
> **But the good ones I've seen**
> **So seldom are clean**
> **And the clean ones so seldom are comical.**

If you are not reasonably funny or clever with your phone message, do not hesitate to throw it out. On the other hand, recognize that what is humorous or clever to one person may not be to another, so discount selective dismay among your callers. If you don't, you may have nothing left to use!

The few limericks and four-liners I have written that have survived fall into several categories that allow for variety and appropriate attention to the seasons of the year. Hopefully, they will give you an idea or two for writing your own.

❧ Seasons

A poem relating to the season at hand is always a good way to cheer up the caller. Here's one for all seasons:

> **When you give the Martins a call**
> **In winter, spring, summer, or fall;**
> **Please bear with a grin**
> **The fact they're not in,**
> **And leave them a message, y'all.**

That "y'all" touch is always a plus if you live well below the Mason-Dixon line—even if you were born five miles from Canada like I was!

SPRING

As you will see by the following examples, the line "Spring has sprung, and so have we" is a handy one to use for spring phone messages. Note that the next poem was written in honor of friends who live in London, England, and periodically complain about having to pay overseas phone rates to listen to our creations.

> **Spring has sprung, and so have we;**
> **We've taken down our Christmas tree.**
> **This info's cheap, in fact it's free,**
> **Unless, of course, you called L.D.**

We even extended to our friends the courtesy of a four-line poem to save them the phone cost of a limerick fifth line! Alas, our thoughtfulness went unnoticed.

So, we discontinued our thoughtful behavior, which wasn't too difficult, and converted our "spring has sprung" theme to limerick form:

> **Our phone is ringing uselessly,**
> **For spring has sprung and so have we.**
> **It doesn't matter;**
> **Record your chatter,**
> **And we'll call back real soon, you'll see!**

(Pause—and then say before the tone) "If you believe that, I have some stock you might ..." (tail off).

Here's a four-liner for late spring. Keep in mind that at this time of year, Texans prepare for several months of oppressive heat:

> **June is here, and May has fell;**
> **Summer's near and it's hot as ... well**
> **You thought I'd say it to make it rhyme,**
> **But that verbal slip I caught in time!**

(Before the tone) "Leave a warm message ..."

SUMMER

Texas summers are so hot, it is difficult to be absurd while writing about them in limerick form.

> **Alas, it's one hundred degrees;**
> **We'll suffer until the next freeze.**
> **The sweat on our brow**
> **Would float a big scow.**
> **Please blow a breeze with your sneeze.**

Note the internal three-word rhyme in the fifth line; that's a plus while you struggle with the thought that you have asked somebody you may not know to sneeze in your face, not that it's anymore pleasant when it is someone you know! Better you should suffer from the heat.

Check the following four-liner and learn that Texans can suffer a negative personality change, or a case of the nasties, when July and August roll around.

> **Ah, here you are on old Ma Bell**
> **And being summer, it's hot as ... well**
> **It's time to tell with tone and all,**
> **Why on earth you made this call!**

The next four-liner was popular, probably because it was short.

**Our summer's here
And so are you.
It's such a shame
That we're not, too.**

(Before the tone) "Chin up, at least we haven't moved!"

FALL

Fall is a great season for phone messages. There are so many things going on requiring our absence that practically everyone we know has a chance to memorize our recorded thoughtfulness, such as:

**Fall is a wonderful time of the year,
Full of pumpkins, football, and beer.
But we continue to gag
On telephone tag.
Do I make myself perfectly clear?**

"The bell tones for thee ..."

Although a wonderful season, the Texas fall is blighted with pollenitis that allergizes us each in our own way. We would be amiss not to have a message dealing with this atrocious phenomenon.

**The pollen that falls in the fall
Makes sniffles for one and for all.
We cough and we wheeze
And sneeze, if you please;
So speak up when you finish this call!**

(Before the tone) "Achoo! ..."

WINTER

For some reason, there is only one poem for winter in our collection, perhaps reflecting the fact that it is our shortest season in Texas.

> **Winter is here, but we are not;**
> **An empty house is what you've got.**
> **So if you want to talk to us,**
> **Please leave your name without a fuss.**

Actually, it is best to refer to the seasons on your answering machine only about one-fourth of the time during the year. Frequently, there are more interesting things to dwell on, as we shall soon see.

❧ Holidays

Holidays are always a good thing to relate to in your phone message. The only downside—you have to change your message as soon as the holiday ends. There's nothing more upsetting than having to endure a "Ho, ho" on January 3, when you call an absent acquaintance and are in the midst of paying Christmas bills.

Here is a message for November–December referring to the banal activity that goes on even before the holiday season begins—a phenomenon that seems to lengthen each year, perhaps encouraged by Christmas advertising that starts as early as July and college football that is aimed all fall long at filling post-season holiday bowls ad infinitum.

> **Grog season is here all aglow,**
> **And we're sorry we can't say hello;**
> **It's the reason we're gone**
> **From now until dawn,**
> **So record your voice mail r-e-a-l s-l-o-w!**

Occasionally, we used another version of this theme:

> **The ho-ho season is here,**
> **So drain a cup of good cheer.**
> **At the tone please don't shout**
> **'Cause the Martins are out;**
> **Just state your piece soft 'n' clear.**

Following are some possibilities when the Christmas season finally arrives—urging the caller to maintain a cheerful holiday attitude even though you're not in:

> **Do you feel out of sorts**
> **And need a big lift?**
> **Then put down the phone,**
> **Write a card, wrap a gift.**

(Before the tone) "Happy Holidays, for heaven's sake!"

> **No need to feel melancholy**
> **With Christmas trees and red holly;**
> **And feeling chagrin**
> **Because we're not in**
> **Is sheer folly, by golly, so solly!**

"Listen for the happy tone ..."

We have yet another Christmas limerick that uses the folly, golly, solly, rhyme routine in a different manner. Once again, there is nothing wrong with repeating successful techniques in your limericks, as long as the limericks tell a unique story, or the same story in a unique way. For example:

> **The holiday holly is jolly,**
> **And we'll sing hello, Dolly, by golly;**
> **The parties are on**
> **So, of course, we are gone.**
> **To think we'd be home is sheer folly!**

(Before the tone) "So solly ..."

Once Christmas day is past, it is time to shift gears immediately to the New Year's celebration that is just ahead. This is a great time to remind your callers that while your new year resolutions called for you to stay at home and answer the phone in person more frequently, you have obviously failed to keep them. Otherwise, your message would not be heard.

The Martins have resolved for this year
To be there much less than they're here.
So it's a pity you see
That you've found only me;
For their lack of resolve, shed a tear.

(Before the tone and tearfully) "And leave a message …"

We used the following version a year or so later:

Austinites, Texans, lend us your ear,
As we enter this glorious and happy New Year.
If you think we have changed,
You're slightly deranged
For a poem, and not us, you'll still hear!

(Before the tone) "So leave another message …"

The following limerick is really a spring-oriented poem that can be used in the seasonal category. However, it is converted—at least for one day—to a holiday limerick with a surprise tag line before the tone.

Spring flowers peep over their pot;
The rains are making things rot.
With the birds give a cheer,
Even though we're not here
For actually we're home quite a lot!

(Before the tone) "Ha-ha, April Fool!"

This was a real favorite among our regular callers, some of whom called one or two extra times to find out what was going on. On the very rare occasions when we have a memorable limerick, our callers will encourage people we don't know to call and listen to it. This is fine if we are still not at home, but if we are, it leads to awkward discussion at best with unknown people struggling to explain why they are calling.

There are other holidays you can play with in your phone messages, such as Halloween and the Fourth of July. Ones to steer away from include Easter, Labor Day, and presidential birthdays. If you're like Tim "the Tool Man" Taylor and don't mind sticking your finger in light sockets, you might take those occasions on. Best, however, to leave politics and religion alone when poking fun in semi-public.

⚠ Caller Frustration

Occasionally, you may want to throw in a phone message that recognizes the frustration that at least some of your callers may feel when you're not at home. Here are some samples:

> **If the Martins would only not roam**
> **You would not have to listen to this poem;**
> > **But this isn't your day,**
> > **So listen away**
> **While you complain because we're not at home!**

(Before the tone) "When you've settled down, leave a message ..."

Here is a four-liner that frequently provided a laugh to ease the caller's frustration:

> **There you are broken hearted,**
> **Your conversation hardly started;**
> **And learning now as you did then**
> **That alas the Martins are gooone again!**

We have noted that frustration is at a higher level during the hot weather months in Texas. The following served to let off steam:

> **When the weather is Texas-red hot**
> **We are gone more often than not;**
> > **But don't fuss and fume**
> > **And steam your perfume.**
> **It's really not worth a whole lot.**

(Before the tone) "Leave a hot message ..."

With the next limerick, we urge our frustrated callers to let the air out:

> Have you ever sat on a thistle,
> And your breath blew out in a whistle?
> If you feel now as then
> 'Cause we're gone again,
> At the tone launch a missile epistle!

Occasionally, when your limerick deals with caller frustration, you might suggest they seek outside help, such as:

> Have you ever felt like climbing a wall,
> Or running and screaming down a long hall?
> Do you feel that way now
> Wishing we're home somehow?
> If so, see your doctor before your next call!

(Before the tone) "Because we won't be home then, either ..."

This next limerick borders on the dangerous, for it provides the caller with an undesirable solution!

> When it's hot more often than not,
> The Martins are gone quite a lot;
> So on this hot day,
> Sure enough, they're away.
> Don't you wish you could have them both shot?

(Before the tone) "Fire away ..."

Do not make frustration a steady diet on your phone messages; too much of a good thing may convince at least some of your callers to be really frustrated and find little humor in what you have to say.

❧ Frequent Absence of the Called

Many of your phone messages will allude to your absence, for if you were not absent, the caller would not be listening to the message. There are times, however, when you may want—for the sake of variety—to make your absence the central theme of your limerick or poem. Here are some illustrations:

In the name of heaven, where are we?
Are we off to a tour of Zimbabwe?
Actually, no,
We're just on the go,
Out buying a brand new Ferrari!

Our callers are quite aware that we have never been in Zimbabwe nor have we ever been in a brand new Ferrari, much less one of our own. So obviously, this limerick is designed to emphasize our tendency to be somewhere other than home.

The next limerick tells it like it is:

Our phone is really a pain,
For it rings again and again.
The reason it does
Is simply because
We're off in a car, train, or plane!

Your callers will welcome a Burma Shave–type ditty in place of a limerick now and then for a change of pace. However, you would be surprised at how many will listen to one and later congratulate you on your latest limerick. Ah, so much for the purists among us:

Is anything certain
Beyond death or taxes?
Heck yes, we're gone,
So record your oral faxes.

Here is another four-liner that emphasizes our habit of absence in short order:

The day we're home
The sun will rise,
Not in the east
But western skies!

Our final four-liner in this category was popular; in fact, we left it on the machine for more than four months without hearing any complaints:

> **We're home about one-third of the time;**
> **The trick is to know just when.**
> **That's better odds than the lottery,**
> **So try us again and again!**

(Before the tone) "At the tone, loser ..."

Can't you just see those Burma Shave signs zipping by—perhaps not, if you are under age fifty!

❧ Anti-Technology

Old folks have a lot of fun with this category, but, if done right, it can appeal to the younger set as well. You know how aggravating VCRs, computers, and electronic gadgets can be. Well, answering machines are no exception. To illustrate:

> **Answering machines are the pits;**
> **They'll drive you right out of your wits.**
> **Who wants to hear**
> **That no one is here?**
> **If I had a bomb, I'd blow this one to bits!**

A tad aggressive, perhaps, but even little old ladies cheer when they hear this one. Here's another nasty message:

> **Isn't our voice mail just great?**
> **It gives you something to hate.**
> **If you'd call when we're home**
> **You'd avoid this sick poem;**
> **It's a shame your timing's third rate!**

Here's another one laced with a dose of heavy sarcasm:

> **Hooray, hooray, you've hit the jackpot;**
> **Our marvelous voice mail is what you've got.**
> **So hide your chagrin**
> **And mail your voice in—**
> **Isn't it great what God hath wrought?**

A final entry in this category turned out to be far more acceptable to our callers than we expected. Maybe it's the tag line that saves it:

If we agree voice mail is great,
Why does it make us so irate?
The answer's simple, for when we hear it,
We know the voice is not flesh, but spirit!

(Before the tone) "Your turn, Casper ..."

☙ **Poking Fun**

Yet another form of humor to help provide variety for your phone answering messages is poking fun at the caller, because he or she can't talk to you in person. This type of message should occasionally poke fun at yourself, the called, for not being able to answer, thereby lessening the possibility of a nasty rebuke on your answering machine. Here are some examples for both the caller and the called, in that order.

AT THE CALLER

We have all shared that sinking feeling when we call someone, and they are not at home. Psychologically, perhaps, it eases the pain when there is a phone message poking fun at us over our dilemma. At least, we tend to believe, the bums recognize how miserable we feel while they are off doing something far less important than staying home to answer our call. Would you feel better, for example, upon hearing:

We cannot get to the phone,
So you're all alone on your own.
If you're sad and not glad
And need us real bad,
Then talk when you hear the (da—) darn tone!

This next message raises the question of whether your call is worth a response, an insult that few recognize to be valid:

As sure as the sun and stars do shine,
You're hooked again on our telephone line.
If you think you're a keeper,
Then wait for the beeper
And tell us if you are Lois' or mine!

Note a couple of things about the above limerick. It has a fisherman theme throughout the message; injecting a theme that has nothing to do with the limerick's basic message is usually a good technique. Also, if you can insert the necessary "Wait for the tone ..." routine in the limerick itself, it reduces the time of your message that the caller must endure. Incidentally, the longer that time is, the funnier your message had better be—for obvious reasons.

For those of you who do not live in the Austin, Texas, area, the name of the reservoir from which we draw our water supply is Lake Travis. You need to know that to appreciate fully the following limerick:

If you run out and water your lawn
Every time you call and we're gone;
Your yard will be wet
From dawn to sunset,
And Lake Travis will be totally drawn!

Using locally known idioms or places in your phone messages is a close call. It allows local callers to relate to you better, which is a plus. On the other hand, your carefully crafted humor may be lost on someone calling from Tibet. Then again, how many people do you know in Tibet?

Our next gem is a touch nasty, but at least it was an improvement (depending on your point of view) over the first version, which my wife vetoed!

Please don't be crude, lewd, or rude;
Your call is being reviewed.
If you're eager to talk,
Then time your sweet squawk
When I've finished transcribing this dude!

This one didn't make it:

> **Please don't be crude, lewd, or rude;**
> **Your call is being reviewed.**
>> **If by any chance**
>> **You have ants in your pants,**
> **You might want to call when you're nude!**

What a priceless gem to put on the cutting room floor! The dual meaning of the fourth line is to die for in conjunction with the fifth line. Besides, wouldn't you want to take off your pants, etc, if your clothing was invaded with ants, especially fire ants?

Here is a four-liner that survived on our phone for six months. Our enthusiasm for it was not even dimmed when we learned recently that the writer who coined the phrase "The call of the wild" did not do well in his selected trade!

> **Is it the call of the wild or the wild that call,**
> **We've never known for sure.**
> **But if you howl when we're not home,**
> **We'll pledge to take the cure!**

(Before the tone) "By staying home, that is ..."

It was frightening to learn how many of our friends and acquaintances used this excuse to howl. Unfortunately, our pledge was not worth the tape it was recorded on.

Callers may have to repeat their call a time or two to appreciate fully the next message. It borders on being too long and too convoluted for easy and quick response. Nevertheless, you will find, should you succumb to limerick writing, that the temptation to find rhyming words for such words as "buckles" overwhelms common sense on occasion. Here it is, for whatever it is worth:

> **Do you notice how a flower stem buckles,**
> **From the weight of a bee while it suckles?**
>> **If you do, you'll feel dizzy**
>> **Like when our phone's busy**
> **And the hand on your phone has white knuckles.**

(Before the tone) "Calm down at the tone . . ."

Now let's turn the tables for a moment and poke fun on us who are being called.

AT THE CALLED

This four-liner pokes fun at my wife and me for not having that modern instrument, the cellular phone, constantly installed at our side:

> **We take no calls in our airplane;**
> **We have no phone in our car.**
> **There is no line to our bathroom,**
> **So hello from wherever we are!**

"P.S. We don't have an airplane, either."

The following limerick raises the perfectly sensible question: Why do we pay for a telephone when we are never at home to use it? (We hear you screaming, "Buy a cell phone!" but we yell too hard at people who phone while driving to do the same thing!)

> **Would you believe we pay for a phone**
> **And then leave it at home all alone?**
> **Like a child out to college,**
> **Our phone thirsts for knowledge;**
> **So give what you've got at the tone!**

(Before the tone) "Gossip, that is . . ."

Here is an example of tying your poem to current events, such as rising interest rates. Since most things, including the economy, are cyclical in nature, you can store your gem when things change and give it an acceptable re-run when they change back again.

> **The Fed keeps raising interest rates**
> **To cool our economy.**
> **When our spending finally satiates,**
> **Then we'll be home, you'll see!**

(Before the tone) "What, you don't buy that?"

cx **Pets**

Our final category of phone messages is directed to pet lovers who leave their pets at home during brief absences. We had a lovable cat, Wedgie, who willingly put up with the messages directed at her and her modest mental abilities. Here are a couple for you to peruse:

> **You may think this ditty's not witty,**
> **For there's no one home but the kitty;**
> > **If you're hardly amused**
> > **And feel somewhat abused,**
> **Leave a message to stir up our pity!**

> **The cat is home all alone**
> **And may not answer the phone.**
> > **In case that is true,**
> > **It's incumbent on you**
> **To talk at the sound of the tone!**

You know, we always felt that Wedgie would do that someday—answer the phone, that is. That would be more than we have done in some time—maybe the next time you call, we'll answer. Ha!

cx chapter three:
family, friend, & acquaintance celebrations

Defining moments in the personal history of family and friends frequently call for a moment of gayety that limericks and four-liners can provide. There are exceptions—terminal illness and funerals rarely lend themselves to lighthearted treatment, even when our current or former existence is celebrated on those occasions. And, oddly enough, application of the limerick to the wedding process is difficult unless done at the bachelor dinner or wedding shower stage. Even though the wedding itself is perhaps the most enjoyable event in our lives, it is a deadly serious event that does not lend itself to poking fun or ridicule. Finally, participation in court cases is usually something we do not want prolonged in print!

With that said, let us explore the use of limericks and four-liners in other key events in our lives.

cx Birthdays

We have been blessed with a grandchild, who has helped keep us up-to-date in various ways. For example, it is through her that we learned that many of today's teenagers prefer the pickup truck for their first vehicle (it was my first vehicle, too, but certainly not my preferred vehicle, since I used it to haul manure on the farm while working summers as a teenager!). So we commemorated her sixteenth birthday thusly:

> **Our sweet Dawn Bell is sixteen**
> **And is licensed to drive a machine.**
> **A Ford truck it is,**
> **By golly, gee whiz;**
> **She'll drive here—there—and between!**

A year later was yet another happy birthday occasion for Dawn. She became seventeen three days before she and her trombone were to appear with her high school band in the New Year's parade in Pasadena. My fax to her in California read:

> **You're seventeen now, so blow your horn;**
> **Congrats—you're a perfect ten.**
> **It won't be long—about three days—**
> **When you'll blow your horn again!**

It is hard to believe that this doggerel made her keepsake file, but at least it helped make her day away from home.

Attainment of age thirty has always been looked upon by the young as the threshold to yesterday, an occasion calling for a touch of philosophic thinking. An employee of mine was having a particularly difficult time with the event, so we eased her burden with a touch of timeless philosophy:

> **Age thirty is really not old;**
> **At least that's what we've been told.**
> **So wear with a grin**
> **The year that you're in**
> **And put future birthdays on hold!**

My wife and I are only eight hours apart in age, so we celebrated our fortieth birthdays in style, complete with a mock funeral and tour of the cemetery. That was a fun birthday, funnier, perhaps, than the fortieth birthday of our younger daughter, when we suddenly realized that everyone in our immediate family had crossed that momentous threshold. Her married name is Bell, which made the following possible:

> **Nancy is forty and all is well,**
> **So let us all celebrate.**
> **We now can call her old Ma Bell,**
> **'Cause she got that name from her mate!**

What that amounted to was laughter through the tears.

A niece of ours married a perennial youth named Lance. On her fortieth, the following was called for, or at least some of us thought so.

> **A lady named Barbara Winn**
> **Faced forty with a fabulous grin;**
> > **When her Lance looked askance,**
> > **She said with sharp glance,**
> **"To grow old is hardly a sin!"**

We have a friend of long standing named Diane. Her fiftieth birthday party took place several months prior to Princess Di's untimely accidental death; thus, it was with an eerie feeling that I came across in my notes for this book the following:

> **We think our queen Di is real nifty,**
> **But our eyes have turned a touch misty;**
> > **For our sweet Lady Royal**
> > **To whom we're still loyal**
> **Has attained the incredible age fifty!**

Would that both could have done so.

On a happier note, in recognizing one of our own milestones, my wife and I welcomed our excellent health at the mutual age of sixty-five:

> **This year the Martins reached sixty-five**
> **And are happy indeed to be alive.**
> > **In a year without pain**
> > **Good health and luck reign;**
> **They've learned first-hand how to thrive!**

At that age, we'd only begun to fight. Our close friends, Chrys and Sarah, attained age eighty without a struggle. Chrys was first, and in recognition of his love for American history, it seemed fitting to paraphrase Lincoln's Gettysburg Address, in honor of his eightieth:

> **Four score and zero years ago,**
> **Chrys' parents brought forth on this continent**
> **a new baby,**
> **conceived in liberty and dedicated**
> **to the proposition that all men are created.**
> **Now we are engaged in a great civil debate,**
> **testing whether that baby**
> **or any baby so conceived and so dedicated,**
> **can long endure.**
>
> **We are met in remembrance of that debate and in**
> **recognition of our finding do cry: Long live Chrys,**
> **who shall not perish from the earth . . ."**

"P.S. The world will little note, nor long remember, what we say here (etc.)."

The four-liner format was used to recognize Sarah's eightieth:

> **Four times twenty blackbirds make a birthday pie,**
> **And ladies who are eighty are very apt to lie;**
> **But Sarah and her songbirds are proud**
> **octogenerians,**
> **For they are known both far and wide as**
> **young regaletarians!**

Here is a final birthday entry for the black sheep of the family (at any age), who is known as a bit of a rake or is simply a relative, preferably distant, who does things differently!

> **Raisin' cane when you are able**
> **(Like rolling dice across a table),**
> **Is a mortal sin**
> **To your kith and kin;**
> **So do it under a phony label!**

"Have fun on your birthday, wherever you are. And while you're at it, please stay there!"

ೕ Graduations

This section is brief, for we have only one grandchild, and everyone else in the family had graduated from their schools long before this poem craze began. Our granddaughter recently finished high school and is now attending Texas A&M University (TAMU). Her love for animals will presumably dictate her training and future career and, therefore, influenced the poems presented in her honor at various occasions following high school graduation. To illustrate:

> **Some of Dawn's animals are shaggy,**
> **While others have tails that are waggy.**
> **LHS* and FFA***
> **Have pointed her way**
> **To a career in which she'll be an Aggie!**

*Leander High School and Future Farmers of America.

Should you try your hand at recognizing family graduation events with such doggerel, it is reasonably easy to inject a secondary theme in the overall graduation theme that alludes to special interests or talents of those being honored.

A four-liner that accompanied a monetary gift for the graduation relies on a play on words to tie in with both the graduation theme and the secondary theme involving Dawn's love for animals:

> **If you've never heard it, you're hearing it now;**
> **There's a quarter horse and, yes, a cash cow.**
> **Putting them together produces strange change**
> **That perhaps will help pay for your home on the range!**

The following limerick poked a little lighthearted fun at Dawn during a family gathering preceding her departure:

ೕ julian g. martin

> **Soon Dawn will leave for T-A-M-U**
> **To learn more about what she'll have to do;**
> > **And while she is there,**
> > **She'll be under the care**
> **Of upperclassmen, counsellors, and animals (!), too.**

For those of you thinking seriously of drafting your own limericks and four-liners, you might note a technique in the above limerick that can be tricky when reciting it. To make things fit, you must spell out T-A-M-U. A little rehearsing beforehand will reveal the need to do this, but keep in mind the next time you see capital letters in a limerick, you may have to pronounce them in various ways to maintain tempo in your verse.

At yet another party before she left, we wanted to alert Dawn to the fact that there is a lot more to college life than simply going to class and learning about animals and their care. So she learned from the following:

> **We salute our beautiful Dawn,**
> **And do say before she is gone:**
> > **"While the purpose of college**
> > **Is all about knowledge,**
> **It's a great place to find a Don Juan!"**

೧ Settling In

After graduation, career selection, and marriage, young couples of today impatiently wade through apartments, condos, and rental housing to build or buy and enter a new house. At a housewarming for a young couple of our church recently, we presented a limerick that recognized while living together with one's spouse is the most important thing in a marriage, a new house certainly doesn't hurt matters!

> **A home is more than a house.**
> **It's a place you share with your spouse.**
> > **But it's neat to have new**
> > **A house with a view**
> **And no hint of a louse or a mouse!**

This jewel did not end up framed and hung on a wall in the new house, but it did serve to lighten the proceedings during its dedication.

In this modern, mobile world of ours, some young couples find the settling-in process is far more complicated than just buying or building a new house down the block from parents or in-laws. While some couples may prefer the complications, others find moving to a new way of life to satisfy the demanding requirements of careers and so on to be a real chore. Return to our church again for an example of a warm-blooded southern couple who had to move north:

> **New Jersey is northeast of Austin**
> **And just barely southwest of Boston.**
> **Where the Nottinghams go**
> **There'll be lots of snow,**
> **And their car will have the defrost on!**

A recent survey of our close friends in Austin revealed that three out of five didn't know how to turn their car's defrost on; one out of five did not know they had a defrosting mechanism. On top of that, another one out of five did not have a defrosting mechanism. (None of this is verified, but you get the picture.)

Visiting Relatives

A few years ago, we were visiting relatives in Ohio, who, in turn, had three relatives who lived on a nearby farm. Their first names were Kye, Kerrey, and Kyle. What a set-up this was—a great opportunity for an alliteration-based four-liner to establish a link with new-found relatives. The following recognition was irresistible, unfortunately:

> **Kye, Kerrey, and Kyle killed kale in their kiln**
> **'Kause it made their kows kough and kollapse;**
> **Krummy kale was also korrupting their krops,**
> **Krowding out korn, karrots, and small mushroom kaps!**

Of course, there is a certain amount of risk in this sort of thing, for it may elicit heartfelt groans and perhaps more serious negative response from those you are trying to "kultivate." (Sorry.)

If you want to score brownie points with relatives who are a bit closer and more meaningful to you, devise a limerick that draws attention to their attributes and your admiration. We have three grandnieces in Utah who are perfect candidates for this treatment. These three talented, attractive young ladies with a strong religious background are the products of the Child and Wesler families, joined in marriage via their parents. So the poem reads:

> **We're related to three wonderful Utes,**
> **Who are known as three talented beauts.**
> > **So let's sing a hymn;**
> > **For Suzanne—Jackie—Kim;**
> **We're so proud of the Child-Wesler offshoots!**

A poem of this nature is helpful at family gatherings and is also a good device to help relieve the inevitably tedious copy found in many family histories—more on the latter problem in Chapter Six.

೮ Anniversaries

One of the best family-friend milestones to apply your poetic talents to is the anniversary, unless you want to leave that sort of thing strictly to Hallmark, et al. And the more advanced the anniversary the better, for you have more background upon which to build. This is not to say you should paw over the closet skeletons in your search for material; this would guarantee a narrowed circle of acquaintances and a sharp reduction in anniversary invites! The following examples applying to our own acquaintances emphasize, for the most part, positives; this does not imply, however, that there were negatives to consider. We only know superb people! Nevertheless, their last names (where used) are camouflaged to protect the innocent! To wit:

> **Twenty-five years of Leon and Zee**
> **Is an absolutely fabulous history.**
> > **Their fine Tejano heritage**
> > **Has given their super marriage**
> **A true touch of class and an air of mystery!**

Yet another parking lot item, drafted while waiting to enter a festive anniversary party:

> **To each other, the Adams are beholden,**
> **For their time together has been golden;**
> > **With a fifty-year seal,**
> > **Their closeness is real**
> **As their love, since biblical times olden.**

Note that the fifth line borders on the irreverent for several reasons, not the least of which is the implied age of the honored. But keep in mind that if you are not a close relative, you will not be invited to a golden wedding anniversary party unless you are a contemporary or older, because no bride in her right mind will surround herself with youth at such a moment. Therefore, you may attack age with impunity, for the simple reason that you share it.

When you have a chance to make a play on words involving the name of the honored, take it:

> **Many people get old and grey**
> **While our Grays never get old;**
> **They've been together for fifty years,**
> **But retain their youthful mold.**

It is inevitable that providing doggerel for a steady stream of friends celebrating their fiftieth will eventually deal with the obvious and fortuitous absence of divorce, particularly when parents are involved. This theme took two limericks for the following couple:

> **Ah, Frances and George are "one thing";**
> **United they stand—Queen and King.**
> > **That their reign is fifty**
> > **Is extraordinarily nifty;**
> **Why, their dynasty's older than China's Ming!**

> **They serve as a symbol for others,**
> **Who seek to be long-term lovers.**
> > **A half-century is theirs;**
> > **Were it true for all pairs,**
> **Particularly fathers and mothers!**

For those who think fifty-year marriages are an act of desperation, read this:

> **A couple of friends, Marilyn and Ben,**
> **Served fifty years in the marital pen.**
> **When asked by friends whether**
> **They've enjoyed life together,**
> **They replied, "We'd do it all over again!"**

✃ Illness

Moderate illness, more than anything else in one's experience, creates a captive audience that you should utilize while you have the chance. We're not talking maudlin behavior here, but a priceless, albeit brief, opportunity to peddle your creative wares to someone who will actually listen. This is the case whether you are ill (or injured), or whether your listener is. For example, a few years ago I had major back surgery and wrote:

> **My back is now back in place**
> **Embraced by a six-month back brace.**
> **So, while the back mends,**
> **I thank our good friends**
> **Whose kindness has helped pain erase.**

The following message was presented to a friend who narrowly escaped death in an accident:

> **You know, it's simply not time for George**
> **To gather the fruits of heaven and gorge;**
> **His stay down on earth**
> **Has achieved second birth.**
> **Now he knows how they felt at old Valley Forge!**

Note that the second line of this limerick deserves punch-line status normally preserved for the fifth line. You cannot always work these things out perfectly, but the limerick served its purpose anyway.

On rare occasions, you can really tell it like it is when you have an afflicted friend who has a great sense of humor and is not too sick or damaged to use it. An appropriate acquaintance provided me with this priceless opportunity a few years ago when she fell and cracked her pelvic bone. A derivation of her name sufficed to create this limerick, which she had posted in her hospital room for visiting ministers to read:

> **A horny old gal named Murelvis**
> **Went to bed with a crack in her pelvis.**
> > **she had to slow down**
> > **In her hospital gown**
> **And stop moves reminiscent of Elvis!**

ᴄ℻ **Retirement**

In the old days, retirement and old age were hardly joking matters. They were taken very seriously, probably because people did not live near as long as they do today. Now retirement offers a second or third career, reasonably good health, and a long tenure of enjoyment or hope that allows for the humorous, and even racy, touch for the retirement occasion. The following "Ode to an Old Man" is in honor of senior male citizens who have achieved this status:

> **One hardly becomes real euphoric,**
> **When he realizes he is historic.**
> > **But it's really okay,**
> > **For he'll find every day**
> **That his candle still has a warm wick!**

Another version of this theme was supplied at a retirement party honoring friends who moved to the farm for their second career:

> **Mary and Bob are on their way**
> **To the land of corn, alfalfa, and hay.**
> > **This trip to the farm**
> > **Has retirement charm,**
> **So enjoy a hot day in your hay if you may!**

You can imagine an inappropriate substitution for the word "day" in the fifth line, which was actually used at the party.

My brother Steve and his wife Lisa had outstanding careers in Vermont public service, he in the state court system and she in the legislature. At the time of their recent retirement, we agreed not to carry on ad nauseum about it all. Instead, we summarized our feelings in a limerick for them "to treasure and place in their memorabilia relating to their retirement:"

> **Will Vermont crime now enjoy a reprieve**
> **And thieves have an ace up their sleeve?**
> **We hardly think so**
> **For the law is on go**
> **Despite the retirement of Lisa and Steve!**

Certainly distinguished careers deserve more respect than that—what else can we say?

ೞ **Potpourri**

There are many informal occasions when a verse comes in handy. For example, we frequent a restaurant that supplies paper tablecloths, crayons, and the waitperson's name to doodle over while waiting for the food. A sample of the resulting doggerel that helps put the waitperson in a good mood:

> **We have a waiter named Scott,**
> **Who wants us to order a lot.**
> **He fills up our plate**
> **With food he thinks great;**
> **We hope that our blood doesn't clot!**

On a higher plane, although not much, we submitted the following entry in a limerick contest for pets on behalf of our beloved cat, Wedgie, a few years ago:

> **Our Siamese, "Wedgie," is sweet sixteen,**
> **A mean and lean arthritic queen.**
> **Her motion once perpetual**
> **Is now barely perceptual,**
> **But her coat has lost none of its sheen!**

Actually, she was sweet and not mean, but I damaged her reputation for the sake of preserving a desired internal rhyme in the limerick. This grubby behavior assured that someone else would win the contest, and so it came to be.

One year, in an effort to lighten the annual plea of our community classical music station for operating funds, the following limerick was offered:

> **Procrastinators put off**
> **Like their cousin, the hideous sloth,**
> > **Their overdue pay**
> > **To KMFA**
> **For funds to serve up musical broth!**

What a questionable way to meet one's obligations to community service, but the station enjoyed the limerick, nevertheless—the second line in particular.

In an effort to help the Salvation Army in its worthy cause that supplies needy children with gifts from Santa during the holiday season, we submitted the following for their publicity campaign:

> **Doesn't grog season make you just gag?**
> **Don't holidays make your heart sag?**
> > **Well, it could be much worse**
> > **If you had to rehearse**
> **Playing Santa with a big, empty bag!**

Needless to say, this offering was rejected without comment.

During my career, we had the opportunity to hobnob more or less superficially with politicians of all persuasions representing various levels of government throughout the nation. One of them was faced with raising funds for re-election to a statewide utility commissioner post in North Dakota, which prompted the following sage advice:

> **Politicians throughout North Dakota**
> **Have trouble fulfilling their quota.**
> > **Population's not there,**
> > **So voters are rare,**
> **And are moved by not one iota!**

We thought the limerick was funnier than he did.

When our children were young, I used to tease them with the fact that the older we all got, the higher their age to mine would be percentagewise. Our older daughter took this quite seriously.

When my daughter Debbie was three,
She was one-eighth my age twenty-three.
By twenty she was half
Forty—two-thirds—such math,
And now she is older than me!

Go figure!

⊂≈ chapter four:
group
situations

Thus far in the book, you have learned a little something about how to write a limerick and how to apply it to practical use. Some of you may have already proceeded to write your own verse, while the rest of you have hopefully been entertained at arm's length! Now we are ready in Chapter Four to go a step further. Here we shall discover how the limerick may be used as a mixer device for captive audiences, groups of people who have been together long enough to know each other by name and other pertinent information.

To apply this practical use of limericks and and an occasional four-liner, you, of course, must be able and willing to present them orally—either as a stand-up entertainer, a host, or a master of ceremonies. If you don't want to do that, you can team up with someone who will and provide that person with the written material. Either way, you have opportunity for expression that can be a lot of fun.

This application does require some extra homework, for in addition to drafting limericks and so on, you must learn all you readily can about the members of the group. The reason for this is that you want to try and include at least a portion of everyone's name in the poetry in as clever a manner as you can devise. Techniques may include a play on the person's name, revealing some fact relating to the person's back-

ground, using a rhyming sequence involving career and outside interests, or exploring the person's relationship to the group at hand.

To avoid an aura of showing off or being too cutesy using this technique, it helps to start the presentation with some self-deprecating
humor. For example, much to the horror of my family and a vast major-
ity of my friends and acquaintances, I love Spam in various forms. To
me, it approaches a status of delicacy that transcends most normal
palates. So, among my various self-deprecating interludes, I have
included the following dealing with my questionable culinary taste:

> **There was a strange old man from Munch**
> **Who frequently ate brunch for his lunch.**
> > **He'd open his Spam**
> > **And calling it ham,**
> **Would serve it with raspberry punch!**
>
> **If you think Spam and punch are real good,**
> **You don't know too much about food.**
> > **It's a mass that will pass**
> > **With considerable gas**
> **And believe me, that's terribly lewd!**
>
> **So the old man from Munch said, "Oh, my;**
> **I'll wash this mess down with Mai Tai.**
> > **Should the rum make it taste**
> > **Like a lunch cooked in haste,**
> **I'll switch to a soda and rye!"**

When you have your audience feeling sorry for you, then you are in
business and ready to proceed. Here is some selected material that
was used in presentations before holiday or vacation groups, church
or social groups, and class reunion groups. Names have been
changed to protect the innocent—most notably the author!

‍ Vacation Groups

Danube Boat Tour

In 1989 my wife and I, together with friends, went on a three-week
cruise of the Danube organized by Stanford University. During the trip,

we became reasonably well acquainted with most of the participants. I began thinking of ways that would help us remember them in the future without conducting endless correspondence, a process that is reserved for only the closest of friends. (Definitely in my case!) During rest periods, I began experimenting with limericks that would include names of my fellow travelers, linking them with the activities and places we shared during the tour. Several little tricks involving limerick construction made this project feasible, even to the extent of finally including all seventy of the tour members.

The most fruitful trick of all for this advanced use of the limerick is to search for first or last names of your subjects—as well as tour activities and geographical features—that rhyme. Why, you ask? Rhyming words are the key to success in this endeavor, for construction of the limerick lines and theme will follow quite easily if the rhyme is set. Other tricks include the use of participant background information relating to your subjects, their exercise habits, their home location, and unique things they did during the tour to help develop the limerick theme.

For purposes of this book, only a few of the limericks and four-liners that were required to cover the entire Danube group are included. Why, you might ask? The important thing to remember when you write limericks for this purpose is that the public at large finds such material to be less than entertaining. Its use should be limited to presentation at tour closing ceremonies or insertion among participant keepsakes of the trip for future reference.

A few of the "Danube" limericks are presented here to illustrate some of the tricks used to include the participants.

Although the trip was ostensibly organized by Stanford University for alumni only, others could participate by paying dues and joining "Big Red's" ex-student association. So I opened my presentation of limericks involving all of the cruise participants by poking fun at those of us who had not attended Stanford:

> **The Wilsons and Martins are fakes**
> **When paying Big Red alum stakes.**
> **Their credentials are phony**
> **And full of bologne,**
> **But so are Phil's, George's, and Jake's.**

Side trips from the Danube and exercise equipment on-board ship provided appropriate rhyming material for several tour participants. The following two limericks are examples:

> **Through lands of Lenin and Marx**
> **Moved Minton, Harris, and Parks.**
> > **McLarren and Pugh**
> > **Went with them, too,**
> **Touring cities, churches, and parks.**

> **Jane and Mary Nicole**
> **Enjoyed a mountainous stroll,**
> > **While Daniel's Christine**
> > **Liked a bicycle machine**
> **To stay thin, an admirable goal.**

Alliteration and the old law firm routine disposed of three more couples on the tour:

> **Haller, Hilliard, and Hind**
> **Are surely not three of a kind.**
> > **A law firm they're not,**
> > **Nor a corporate plot;**
> **It's a Stanford tour where they bind!**

Three individuals in the tour group were chosen to lead a German band during one of the social events and indicated they enjoyed music more than art. Fortunately, one of them had the unusual nickname of "Hoov"—short for Hoover—which allowed this limerick to work:

> **Hester, Nieman, and Hoov**
> **Are all well traveled and smooth.**
> > **They direct foreign bands**
> > **In faraway lands,**
> **But would not last long in the Louvre!**

Finally, recognition was granted to our outstanding "crew" of three professors and two administrative assistants—Lena and Kathy—who gave the trip so many defining moments. Not only did the crew deserve recognition during closing ceremonies, but it also gave the author an outside chance to get his material into the University archives. However, do not bother to call to confirm this.

> **Professors Simmons and Mishka named Anne**
> **To our trip gave a touch of élan.**
> > **While Lena corralled**
> > **And Kathy cajoled**
> **To keep us according to plan!**

> **A seminar date with Joe Sinich**
> **Was as rich as a dish of creamed spinach;**
> > **His menu? East Europe**
> > **With Danubian syrup**
> **And as timely as England's Point Greenwich!**

ELY, MINNESOTA, ELDERHOSTEL

In recent years the elderhostel movement has grown to humongous proportions. A steady flow of elderhostel outings is scheduled throughout the United States and across the world to accommodate thousands of participants who are over the age of fifty-five. Each elderhostel lasts one or two weeks, involving thirty to fifty attendees, as a rule. Usually, there are classes or activities involving three subjects, plus outings that take advantage of the unique settings in which the elderhostels are located.

Frequently, an elderhostel will schedule a closing ceremony at which participants may present their observations about the week or weeks just concluded. On rare occasion, I present limericks and four-liners involving all participants, as a recall device to keep an outstanding elderhostel in mind, for after attending a half-dozen elderhostels, recall tends to blur in the absence of visual aides.

In the summer of 1996, my wife and I attended an elderhostel we felt deserved to be remembered in Ely, Minnesota. A combination of canoe and computer instruction in a wilderness setting with some fun participants justified recall.

Again, only a few selections are mentioned here, for the purpose of illustrating how one can contribute to lasting recall, even if poor taste is involved. The following limerick includes new-found friends we wished to remember, along with a brief description of the area in which the hostel was located in northeast Minnesota.

> **Dan and Dee White and Bill and Jan Plummer**
> **Are Ohioans who met just only this summer**
> **At a great place called Ely**
> **That's real touchy-feely,**
> **Where mosquitos are considered a real nasty bummer!**

The next limerick emphasizes the togetherness our small group experienced in the wilderness. However, please note that the second line is not true, but rather a play on words referring to a participant whose name was Gillette and the razor by the same name:

> **Darleen helped Jerry Gillette**
> **By keeping his razor real wet,**
> **While Nelly and Lee**
> **With Jack and Bobbie**
> **Kept company with a Stone named Annette!**

Following is an "Ely" limerick that breaks with reality for the sake of technique—a desired internal rhyme in the second line. Had this incident actually happened, it would have made the limerick an historic gem for that particular elderhostel. As it was, it simply rated a footnote dedicated to nonsense!

> **During food break were Jenny and Walt**
> **Finding fault with the salt in their malt;**
> **Through crocodile tears**
> **They spied Sue and Jim Meers,**
> **Who helped bring their rage to a halt!**

❧ Social Groups

CONSENSUS BUILDING

Adult social group settings, particularly in a church environment, can be quite deadly at times. People tend to take themselves too seriously, when they are thrown together for a purpose that attracts varying points of view. It is incumbent upon the master of ceremonies—should there be one in these situations—to make light of things and encourage participants to laugh either with or at each other as a means to ease the way to solution or consensus.

One such gathering took place in our church a few years ago, and I was called on to MC the situation. The purpose of the meeting, held in social format over dinner, was to create a dedicated fund for church building projects. There were those who strongly wanted it and logically named it after a very popular, hard-working church leader as a means of soliciting winning support. Those opposed did not want church funds to be encumbered any more than absolutely necessary.

Among the introductions and one-liners, I interspersed a few limericks to ease the tension. The following was for our church administrator, who had to operate the fund in question:

> **We'll never let it be said**
> **That "We'd rather be dead than be Jed."**
> **We'd much rather say,**
> **"Jed, you make our day,"**
> **Which amounts to a positive instead!**

This served to draw attention away from the conflict, albeit at the administrator's expense, and shifted the audience into neutral. Next to receive attention in the ceremonial banter was the church leader who was being honored by the project:

> **There once was a lady named Tess,**
> **Who never took no for a yes.**
> **She fought noble rounds**
> **For our church and its grounds**
> **And cleaned up a mell of a hess!**

Finally, to help close debate and finalize the project's funding design, we "honored" the church member who had spearheaded the campaign into reality, saying:

And then there's our own Mrs. Docker,
Who's known to be a fast talker.
    When she moves earth and sun
    To get something done
It's best you don't shock her or mock her!

And guess what? No one did!

⚥ Career Recognition

If you are called upon to participate in a gentle roast for a treasured employee who is leaving after a lengthy, successful career, the limerick can be a useful tool to help review the employee's career and say goodbye. Somehow, whatever else you may have to say melts into the woodwork of forgotten history, while a limerick has a chance to live on even when it doesn't deserve to do so.

When our Director of Music left our church employ after twenty-seven years, the following two limericks excerpted from a series entitled "Twenty-seven Years is Not Enough!" seemed appropriate:

There is a nice lady named Sue,
Who quietly knows what to do.
    Under a minister named Morgan
    We purchased an organ
That she knows how to play thru and thru!

This lass can play mass with such class,
And make sense out of music's morass.
    Her talent's unique
    With a touch of mystique.
It's so sad that from us this will pass.

Nothing more needed to be said, but, of course, there certainly was.

⚥ Class Reunions

If you are master of ceremonies or responsible for mixer agenda at your class reunion, the use of limericks and other poems to recall old times or to bring the class members up-to-date on others who are attending can be effective. Be careful, however, to avoid anything that might prove to be insulting or negative; for example it is best not to use the rhyming words *hearse*, *curse,* and *worse* in a limerick applying to a new widow, no matter how great the limerick might otherwise be!

Also, be sure your audience is reasonably sober and can hear what you have to say, for the simple reason that a good limerick relies on the listener as much as the presenter to make the clever nuances and catch phrases a reality. And believe it, you cannot repeat a limerick at a function or even in private conversation and expect it to go over well. You have only one strike to hit a home run.

In recent years, program-deprived class leaders have asked for limericks to help mix things up for fellow classmates at reunion time. Unfortunately, the results have failed to win an award of any kind!

45TH CLASS REUNION

At this reunion there was no attempt to name everyone in a set of limericks, because the format called for one-liners, hair and age jokes, and other insults. However, there were a few poems interspersed throughout the presentation. A limerick about our MC, who was concerned that classmates might talk too long, started things off.

> **Our hostess is Fancy Mengo,**
> **Who urges we not be too slow.**
> **We must make it snappy**
> **For she'll be unhappy,**
> **If we fail to win, place, or show!**

The fifth line gives the limerick the twist it needs, although the listener needs to be alert enough to realize the connection between a desired fast program and a horse race. (If limerick writers are overly subtle, they lose it, because again—be aware that limericks cannot be repeated or dissected in the telling and remain effective.) This poem was followed by two more limericks urging classmates to keep it short when offered a chance to speak about their lives:

> **Remember, this is not your life:**
> **Don't list the begats with your wife.**
> **When the spotlight's on you**
> **Keep remarks to a few.**
> **Be Marshal Dillon, not Barney Fife!**

Again, a special urging to cut down on the chatter and home in on the good stuff:

> **We don't want to know where you've been**
> **Or whether you drink rum or gin;**
> **Or the make of your car**
> **Or the fact you shoot par;**
> **Just let us in on your sin!**

A few limericks were used to emphasize classmates who did very well for themselves after graduation. One who made her mark in the legal community as a free spirit generally opposed to the stifling bureaucratic mind was lauded thusly:

> **Grace Kirk is one of those lawyers**
> **Who hates bureaucratic annoyers.**
> **She aims fumigation**
> **At their litigation**
> **And lobbies against them in foyers!**

Dr. Lloyd Brennan, a popular philosophy professor, who proved his worth by launching our classmate, Hubert Mendon, into a world-renowned career in theology, was in attendance at the reunion as the only honorary class member we ever had. We tipped our hat to him:

> **Students generally avoid**
> **Santyana, Emerson, and Freud.**
> **Our "Hu" Mendon did not,**
> **And look where he got,**
> **Thanks in part to a Brennan named Lloyd!**

Another way to involve attending classmates is to make a play on their last names. It is surprising how many people have names that can relate to a characteristic they may have. The following classmates provided excellent examples of this phenomenon:

- Harry Glass, who was real smooth.
- Jack Braun, who had a powerful physique.
- Jim Gallant, who certainly was with the ladies.
- Dick Bishop, an ideal alum of a school with
    the motto "Battling Bishops."
- Renee Purdy, who was and is.
- Sherri Comfort, who provided same for her many friends.
- Nicole Swank, who was, even before marrying
    Terry Swank.
- Jasper Marsh—sorry about that, Jasper!

When all the classmates had participated in the fun, a closing limerick was called for:

> **This half-century class is real nifty,**
> **And it has been since year 1950.**
> > **In only five years**
> > **Let's return with our peers,**
> **And celebrate our ever-lovin' fifty!**

FIFTIETH HIGH SCHOOL REUNION

At my fiftieth high school reunion, the mixer format called for including the seventy-eight classmates attending in a series of poems—using their first and/or last names as they were at graduation or after marriage. It took eleven limericks and four four-liners, using history, play on names, geographical location, nicknames, achievements, and personality characteristics, to include everyone. When you feel comfortable with your limerick composition progress, I suggest you try out this technique with small groups that you know personally when you want everyone to become involved and acquainted with each other. It's fun.

Following are a few selections from the reunion limericks, again to show technique in the event you want to try your hand at it. As in the case of vacation and other groups, in-house limericks have little application for outside readers except in that rare instance when a limerick is good enough to transcend the problem of dense content.

Most reunions dwell on those participants who come the farthest to attend. A limerick can appropriately address this subject:

> Five classmates compete for living farthest away.
> Southwest's Martin and Fineberg both have their own say.
>> As do Gary from Montana
>> And Jean from Tarzana,
> But it's Rob from Monaco that carries the day!

Another version of the old law firm routine combined with mention of a common first name is one way to "dispose" of several classmates in one verse:

> Kayjian, Rifland, Tarbo, and Cobb
> Sound like a law firm serving a mob.
>> But it's not law they share
>> Nor the same color hair;
> It's John, a name common as corn-on-the-cob!

Same first names, combined with other more irreverent information, provided the theme for the following limerick:

> Two Freds—Shupi and Lord—we're delighted you're here,
> Along with Claire Russell, a name we revere;
>> And a Timmons named Clarence
>> Who was named that by parents,
> While Singer and Barns share a month we hold dear.*

*June.

Modern medicine and technology may provide a cloak of reality to the four-liner used to close the reunion presentation, a poem that would have been dismissed fifty years ago as sheer, if not cruel, nonsense. Even so, note the tag line that reduces the whole idea to illusion!

> So here we are after fifty years
> With this priceless time to visit
>> our peers.
> And I kid you not, this is no myth;
> I expect to see you on our 75th!*

*If you believe that, the stock mentioned in Chapter Two is still up for grabs!

vocation causes

All of us at one time or another are advocates, presumably because it helps us define purpose in life. Since this is not a philosophical text, suffice it to say we seek various ways in which to express our beliefs— some of us through family, others through organizations aligned with causes, others through chosen avocations, and so on. Some of us are fortunate enough to enhance the enjoyment or meaning of our work careers with advocacy, provided we avoid the trap of single-minded-ness, which closes the door to the rest of what life has to offer!

Whether you agree with that conclusion or not, I have found it is best to search for attractive ways to pursue one's advocacy in the hope that more will listen to one's point of view. One of those ways is the "useful" limerick. During my thirty-eight-year-long affiliation with the Texas independent oil and gas producer, I found that occasionally pok-ing a little fun at the many serious issues confronting the independent both inside and outside his/her industry guaranteed a wider audience, although not necessarily more sympathetic!

Opportunity to apply the limerick in this manner arose during the late 1970s, when—as an association exec—I had a sidebar opportunity to perform as Limerick Editor for *The American Oil and Gas Reporter*, one of the independents' national magazines. This was during the period of overreaction by official Washington to presumed energy shortages caused by periodic conflict in the Mideast—the United States' main source for imported oil. Much of the resulting legislation and regulation simply served to make worse the supply shortfall experienced by the American consumer and provided an excellent breeding ground for good limerick copy.

As you can well imagine, this situation created some red-hot issues that still influence political energy discussions some twenty-five years later! Let's see how some of the published limericks in our magazine added to the heat from the independents' point of view. Before we do that, however, let's take a look at the limerick used to advise my readers, who had been encouraged to submit entries for use, what they could and could not do in print:

> **Entries may quote from the Bible,**
> **Or cast aspersions based on the tribal;**
> **But when you maim fame**
> **By including one's name**
> **Your material constitutes libel.**

A good rule to follow when writing your own material for public digestion.

In the 1970s, as in the 1990s, there was a running debate over what fuels should be allowed, either through regulation or economic manipulation, to serve the lucrative U.S. energy market. Back then, the major debate centered on foreign versus domestic oil supply. (Today, the debate has moved essentially to environmental concerns as they relate to the various types of available fuel and the amounts consumed.) In late 1976, domestic oil producers' concern over the perceived threat of a Washington energy policy favoring displacement of domestic oil supply by cheaper, but less secure, foreign supply spawned the following verse:

> **In politics and football this fall**
> **Is a question of interest to all;**
> **If the name of the game**
> **Is whose fuel to flame,**
> **Will we be the political football?**

Paranoia has a large role to play in Washington activity!

A few weeks later, emphasis shifted to the election process in the continuing search for an energy policy that might favor domestic supply over foreign supply:

> **Will candidates who won in their race**
> **Over those who ran show or place,**
> > **When Congress convenes**
> > **With its new ways and means,***
> **Give energy a policy face?**

*This refers to the House Committee on Ways and Means, which, along with other key congressional committees, had a major role to play in energy legislation development.

During the following winter, Washington was regulating oil prices in various ways, leading to the following observation on economic theory:

> **When you regulate price, I am told,**
> **You diminish petroleum sold.**
> > **Since price is knee-high,**
> > **There is little to buy,**
> **And we are left out in the cold!**

If this eats your heart out, the limerick has done its job. If it makes you vomit, it has still done its job.

Actually, the design of Washington price regulation during the 1976–77 winter helped some categories of oil producers at the expense of other producers. This gave rise to this loaf of wry bread:

> **The crude price rollback takes gall,**
> **For it robs poor Pete to pay Paul.**
> > **This cleat to Pete's seat**
> > **Will deplete and defeat**
> **Our optimum search for petrol.**

Sheer advocacy—or is it ecstasy? Not really, for the price rollback rolled on!

The next limerick has been used in several forums, probably because it is easy to memorize, among other things. However, to be fully appreciated, it must be understood in the context for which it was designed. In 1977 a House oversight committee on natural gas transportation was convinced that the nation's natural gas producers and pipeline companies were holding back offshore production to drive up prices. The producing state energy agencies that controlled production agreed with the industry that this was not true. So this led to a strongly worded defense:

> **The mass of the gas that will pass**
> **Through the nation's pipeline morass**
> **Equals industry production,**
> **Not probers' deduction,**
> **No matter how much they harass!**

A few weeks later, I listened with mixed emotions to a U.S. senator from a gas-producing state, who included the limerick in his text as though it were his own.

In the spring of 1977, energy producers began to realize that official Washington did have an energy policy, after all. The problem was, it was one producers did not like! Ergo, the following limerick went into print:

> **Is our petroleum policy a bit pathetic**
> **Now that government is very energetic?**
> **Or do we need a growing Fed**
> **To control us 'til we're dead**
> **In the hope that life for all might be aesthetic?**

Boiling questions are these and remain unanswered to this day.

In mid-1977, energy was becoming a social issue reflecting President Jimmy Carter's pronouncement earlier in the year that the energy issue was the moral equivalent of war! One of the ways to cope with this development, of course, was to establish a large Department of Energy (DOE) to handle, among other things, the regulation of energy supply and use. Independent producers viewed this move with distrust, which led to the following limerick:

We'll pay a big buck for DOE,
Ten point six billion or so;
    It's a shame this big rack
    On the taxpayer's back
Will only slow energy flow!

Deer hunters throughout the oil patch were especially fond of this analogous verse.

Energy shortages in 1977, caused in part by governmental regulation, led to a blackout in New York City that received wide publicity. Producers used this event to plead for energy policy that would encourage supply; the next limerick helped give expression to the plea.

The blackout in old New York City
Gave a warning more tragic than witty.
    So why can't we learn
    To find fuel to burn
Will take more than Miracle Man Mitty.*

*This was the title of a contemporary broadway show starring Danny Kaye.

In the midst of this energy warfare, The House of Representatives in Washington passed a bill that would recontrol oil prices and initiate new taxes on the industry. Attention was then drawn to the U.S. Senate, where the bill next moved in the legislative process. An appropriate limerick sounded the alarm:

The Orwellian era is now here,
As the House made abundantly clear.
    Decontrol has been axed
    And petroleum taxed.
Please, Senate, strip Big Brother's gear!

Keep in mind, Dear Reader, that these "literary potshots" served only as attention-getters and were never intended to provide the energy industry with sound argumentation for debate purposes.

The illogical nature of Washington's frantic legislative response to energy shortages in the 1970s frustrated the energy industry no end.

This limerick, written during football season, gave expression to that frustration:

> **Would you sub your players with ref'rees**
> **Or serve carrots with parsnips, not peas?**
> **If so, then you'll go**
> **With the energy show**
> **Of D.C.'s, while you freeze, if you please!**

Note the key fifth line of the limerick incorporates a wraparound of the fourth line to complete the basic thought of the limerick begun in the third line. The wraparound also serves to initiate an internal rhyme in the fifth line. (An aside to those of you interested in developing your limerick talent: We must be careful when trying to be clever with our limerick design that we don't hopelessly fog up the meaning of the verse for our readers. We have arrived if we can be clever and clear at the same time!)

At one point in the energy debate, producers were desperate in their attempts to establish sound energy policy from their point of view. A turn to philosophy offered solution:

> **Socrates deep in his tomb**
> **Asks who is ripping off whom.**
> **Were only he here**
> **To make energy clear**
> **With its policy still in the womb!**

Unfair beseeching? Probably, but who said life was fair anyway?

In seeking energy policy that would encourage wider development of the primary energy sources—oil and natural gas—producers tended to question whether alternate fuels could fill the gap economically (or otherwise), if such policy was not forthcoming. You can detect the sneers in the following limerick!

> **When your oil and your gas are all gone,**
> **Turn your windmills and yule logs right on.**
> **While collecting cow chips,**
> **Import garbage in ships**
> **And keep cozy in long underwear drawn!**

See what fun you can have with a limerick that serves a cause.

In early 1978, it became evident that Washington had overreacted to the ongoing energy crisis with onerous legislative and administrative regulation. This next limerick suggested that the moral equivalent of war begun earlier had served its time:

> **If government is responsible for**
> **Roadblocks to production galore,**
> > **Could the President end**
> > **With strokes of a pen**
> **His "moral equivalent of war?"**

No.

Industry irony continued:

> **The ingredients for energy stew**
> **Are the cause of its pungent pew.**
> > **Uncertainty and regs,**
> > **Square holes for round pegs**
> **And politicians, to name just a few!**

April 20, 1977, marked the date of the presidential speech describing the energy issue as the moral equivalent of war. A year later, the anniversary ignited a new wave of concern over the industry's culinary welfare:

> **Now that April twentieth is here**
> **Energy illness has run a full year.**
> > **Is it ptomaine or Potomac***
> > **Poisoning our stomach**
> **While awaiting our Congressional test smear!**

*This is not a reference to Potomac fever, which frequently afflicts those living in Washington.

Nor is it a reference to the water quality of the Potomac River, which runs through Washington. It is an appropriate word referring to the federal government scene that also serves to improve the limerick in association with the words ptomaine and poisoning. (Unfortunately, if you have to explain your limerick and its design, you have not produced an acceptable product for general consumption).

In 1978 congressional reaction to the energy crisis moved to the natural gas-producing industry. A horrendously complicated bill was passed, "The Natural Gas Policy Act of 1978," to regulate natural gas prices at the producer level. In some instances, it took high-powered energy CPAs and tax lawyers to determine what price or prices were legal for the producer's product. This provoked a smart-aleck reaction:

> **Do you know how to play "Price is Right?"***
> **Is your lawyer exquisitely bright?**
> > **You do! He is! Then you may**
> > **Price your gas by the end of the day;**
> **Otherwise, it will take you all night!**

*A popular but undemanding TV quiz show that tested one's ability to guess economic values.

This may be a good time to throw in a reminder for the reader. Generally, a good limerick must be able to stand alone without the need to explain its contents, even in brief footnote form. However, this is not necessarily true for limericks developed to have fun at a reunion or to highlight a cause, as is the case in this chapter. Such limericks will be understood without explanation within the community to which they are directed, but frequently must be clarified for consumption by the general public. So, if you become inclined to write limericks only for private or well-defined groups, don't worry about clarifying anything— just go for it!

One of the main arguments used by proponents of the natural gas legislation mentioned earlier was that it would strengthen the U.S. economy. This led to the following commentary:

> **It hardly takes a Rhodes scholar**
> **To track the decline of the dollar;**
> > **But he's needed to guess**
> > **How the Energy Act mess**
> **Collars the dollar up taller!**

Once again, the fifth line of the limerick is the star of the show.

All major legislation considered and passed by Congress is subject to a ferocious tug of war by opposing sides during the process. The next limerick summarizes this phenomenon:

> **Our move to have Fed regs arrested**
> **Is foiled by interests quite vested.**
> **Whether lawyers in foyers,**
> **Or bureaucratic annoyers,**
> **The road to free market's congested!**

You may recall another version of this limerick in Chapter Four; the lawyer-foyer-annoyer routine is always a good one to work with in different situations.

In a lull during the energy fight in 1979, it was time to gig politicians who closed their minds to the legislative process, which must have give and take to pass anything important. So:

> **The political girdle's fantastic**
> **With its spastic, bombastic, elastic;**
> **But should one tie the cinch,**
> **He's (She's) caught in a pinch**
> **And controlled as tho' draped in hard plastic!**

Keep in mind, however, that the best bargaining tools are in the hands of those who have the courage of their convictions.

When the Natural Gas Policy Act (NGPA) was finally passed into law, producers who disliked the final compromise had to learn to live with it. Thus, it was time for this touch of realism:

> **The trouble with N. G. P. A.**
> **Independent producers do say**
> **Is the complexity of it**
> **Makes them want to shove it;**
> **But damnation, it's here to stay!**

Can't you just hear Rex Harrison singing that ditty onstage in a George

Bernard Shaw play? Well, maybe not. I can imagine Harrison singing it, but I can't imagine Shaw writing it! As a matter of fact, Langford Reed, in his *The Complete Limerick Book*, notes that Shaw joined other authors in the opinion that limericks had to be ribald and unprintable to be any good.

Railing against federal regulation was a favorite pastime for the energy industry during the 70s and early 80s, since the industry was getting so much of it. Although aware that human behavior can run amok in the total absence of shackles, the industry was prone to say enough is enough on occasion. On one such occasion:

> **Regulation is a horrible bind**
> **That persists in besetting mankind.**
> **To control one another**
> **Is a terrible druther,**
> **So Congress, keep that in mind.**

Enough said.

At the end of the 1970s, the energy war in Washington turned again to crude oil and products. A huge excise tax was attached to domestic oil and its products, creating an even greater economic advantage for low-priced foreign oil imported into the United States. This event ushered in the holiday season in 1979 and spawned the following series of limericks:

> **It's time to thank Congress again**
> **For its holiday energy hen.**
> **Such turkey gobble**
> **Creates dollar hobble,**
> **While enhancing marks, rubles, and yen.**

> **This horrible oil excise tax**
> **Swings a vicious and terrible axe**
> **That cuts exploration**
> **Throughout our nation,**
> **Guaranteeing supply mini not max!**

Billions of barrels of oil
Lie under United States soil;
And that's where they'll stay
From each June to each May,
When drilling, by taxing, we foil.

Well, times change, and such overstated threats tend to blend in with the tide of human history. Today, the energy industry is becoming a technological process with environmental concerns that must and are being addressed. A cause or stand in the industry now would require a new set of limericks and someone else to write them. As I said in my last energy related limerick in 1980:

To the relief of many, I'm sure,
This limerick is the last to endure.
New duties of mine
Force me to resign.
It was fun roasting issues on a skewer!

&3 julian g. martin

chapter six:

true short stories
for family history

The extra syllable in the vital fifth line proved my point—it was time to quit!

> **Did your grandfather fight in a war?**
> **Were any of your relatives poor?**
> **Does your sister teach art?**
> **Is your cousin real smart?**
> **Then WRITE—what are you waiting for?**

Few people write a book, a short story, or even a magazine article. But a lot of people write at least a portion of their family history or in some way directly or indirectly help another family member do so. If you are one of them, or just close to one of them, is it possible you might want to help make your family history, with its endless "begats" and graveyard maps, a little more interesting and readable for the generations that follow? If so, I suggest you take this chapter seriously in the hope that you, or whoever writes your family history, will lighten up and pass on a life story worth reading.

If you are like me, your first thought may be, "I don't have anything in my background or experience that is the least bit unusual or interesting." Wrong! The dullest among us with a halfway decent recall mechanism can find something to alleviate the tedium of a written recital describing dates of birth, family moves, and gravestone listings.

In a moment, we shall review a few short stories relating to my background on things humorous, sad, tragic, coincidental, poignant, and, yes, irritating, to prove that an ordinary background can provide such goodies. There is no attempt here to present a full family history in story form—far from it. Rather, the suggestion here is for you to relieve the tedium of straightforward historical recital with inserted vignettes that are based on fact.

Most important of all, you don't have to be a polished author to do this. I have witnessed more than thirty people do this, with little advance notice or preparation, quite successfully. The secret: Speak from the heart, recording or writing down what actually happened as you remember it, and you will have something worthwhile to read—at least by your family members and close friends. (Let's face it, no one else is going to read our family tree stuff, unless we're related to Princess Di.) It is also important to remember that while good writing generally avoids overuse of the "I" word, it is acceptable in family history writing. For this is your story and no one else's.

In addition to the short stories, insert in your family history as you go along little personal items that bring your copy to life. Examples from my own background:

ଓ A Mother's Humor

"Peanut butter is a good winter food item; it provides little sweaters for your teeth!"

ଓ Out of the Mouth of Babes

At the age of six, I looked at the hospital where I was born and said with a burst of innocent pride: "Out of all those babies, my Mommy chosed [sic] me!"

ଓ Born Old

At the age of sixteen, I was asked to escort a divorced lady of thirty-seven and her three bratty children on a day boat-trip into Canada across the Vermont border. It was during World War II. As a Canadian Major was observing the children trying to dismantle the steamer, he turned to me and said: "I know what you're going through; I have three of my own."

❧ Born Old 2

My wife and I met on a blind date at college in 1947. She had always wanted to go out with an older man. I looked the part, particularly since I wore a WWII navy pea coat that belonged to my older brother. Eventually, she discovered that I was younger than I looked. Nevertheless, she did get her wish; I'm eight hours older than she is!

❧ Born Old 3

One day in my sixty-third year, I was waiting to get on the elevator in my office building. I noticed this attractive lady in her mid to late thirties was staring at me. Thinking I might remind her of someone she knew—such as her husband, brother, or even her father—I made the mistake of asking if we knew each other. "Oh, no," she gushed, "you simply remind me of my grandfather. He was such a wonderful old man!"

❧ Just Another Martin

This was a saying for all members of the family once they crossed the family threshold from their supposed accomplishments in the world. It was a saying worth keeping in mind, for example, when we gloried in such ancestry as Governor Richard Warren on the *Mayflower*, and the Roosevelt family. The light dimmed on such reminiscence when we discovered that another member of our historic family, Suzannah Martin, was one of the Salem witches put to death 300 years ago! But what a great item to insert in a boring page of family history.

❧ Name I.D.

I never liked my first name, Julian; I thought the only time it would have validity would be on the front cover of a book I might write some-day. It took me a long time to overcome this potentially serious prob-lem. I went through periods of "Lefty," "Marty," "J.G.," "Hey you," etc., before I came to my senses. My middle name, "Grant," might have been a good substitute, but I have lived most of my life in the South. This foolishness finally stopped one day when one of my most revered association leaders tried to introduce me with this routine: "George, I want you to meet—ah, Mister, ah, ah, Marty; yes, that's it!" Well, it wasn't, and I quickly began a campaign of restoring my identity by using my first name for the first time.

And now for the true short stories.

◌ Getting Even

> There are many ways to even a score,
> Like poking your spouse to stop a bad snore.
> But an eye for an eye
> Will not cure a sty.
> So, stop and count ten—1, 2, 3, 4 ...!

At the age of six, I was reasonably athletic but totally innocent when it came to martial arts. One of my "close" friends, David, was much more advanced in his boxing technique and proved it with a right cross to my mouth during an altercation over play in the Vermont ice and snow in front of his home.

Unfortunately, the blow broke my new "permanent" lower front tooth right where the bite is the hardest. It took six weeks of painful weekly visits to the dentist to drill the tooth down with his 1936 equipment for the installation of a permanent crown. As we shall see, however, this was only the beginning.

Meanwhile, it was not something easily forgotten. For the next three years, I waited patiently for an opportunity to return the favor while learning more about the art of self-defense. Needless to say, I kept this campaign to myself, realizing even at that early age that adult san-ity would interfere with my plans.

At last the chance to restore my "youthhood" and to retaliate came.

We were both attending summer camp when the director announced a wrestling contest. I immediately challenged David, and the next day I won the match, admittedly with less fanfare than I felt the effort deserved.

Alas, in a very real sense I did not win anything. First, retaliation has its limits when it comes to experiencing healthy vindication. More importantly, however, over the next sixty-two years I have experienced periodic pain, frustration and expense with the tooth and its successors. Early on, the cap turned black and stayed that way. Finally, it fell off, and a more modern dentist cleaned the cap, reset the screw, and reinserted the cap. Then the root in which it was inserted gave way after years of hard-bite-pounding pressure. This meant excavation of the worst sort.

Next, the dentist and I tried two versions of insertion bridges, but they were unsatisfactory in their effort to handle the hard bite. Next we tried a Maryland bridge, which essentially attaches to the adjacent teeth. This was better, but the glue attaching the bridge to the adjacent teeth would give away at six months on the dot. After two years of that, the dentist discovered a new, more powerful glue. Hooray, you say! Not so. The glue was so powerful that when one of the attachment teeth moved slightly due to advanced age, a hellacious toothache ensued. This meant dislodging the powerful glue, which took novocaine, three people, and a full morning to disengage.

Not to despair? Depends on your point of view. Several months later, one of the supporting teeth developed a root hickey as the result of all that history of pressure, and guess what. A root canal with all its expense and bother was now necessary. There was a big plus to this process—the operation could be performed without removing the immovable bridge. Alas, there was a big minus as well.

In between root canal visits, my wife and I had scheduled a business-pleasure trip, but all seemed well to proceed. Not so. As we approached the mountainous terrain of northern New Mexico on our way to Santa Fe, the tooth began to sing. During our stay in Santa Fe, it got excruciatingly worse—on a weekend, of course, with no dentist in town available. Finally, on our last day before moving on to Phoenix to visit relatives, it occurred to me that my problem was perhaps caused by the low pressure existing at Santa Fe's 7,000 feet. Realizing that Phoenix is just above sea level, we raced to our destination, and the pain disappeared.

That was the first, and probably the last, time that I have welcomed the topographic blessings offered by Phoenix. Meanwhile, the curse of David lives on until I join him in the tomb.

FORT HOLABIRD MARYLAND

⚮ A Brush with Death

War is hell and most unfair,
Participants quite agree.
Some suffer well beyond their share
And go down in history.

It was late in November 1951, and the Chinese had just complicated the horrible conflict in Korea by crossing the Yalu River virtually unannounced and joining in the deadly fray. At that point my name came up in the draft, on the very day my wife learned that she was pregnant with our first child. I could have pled for deferment under the rules, but decided to serve as my father and older brother had in times past.

My service experience began in Camp Deven in Massachusetts, which—in retrospect—was a little like taking novocaine in the dentist's chair. Bands played, beer flowed, and the food and jovial PR contingent running things were outstanding. "Welcome to the U.S. Army," they said. "You'll find it to be a wonderful home away from home with an opportunity of a lifetime to learn new things and develop new friends." What a hollow statement that turned out to be for most of the recruits at hand.

Soon enough, realism hit and hit hard. Although I had been fortunate enough to be designated for counterintelligence school, I had to first complete infantry training. I was assigned to Fort Dix, New Jersey, for seventeen of the hardest weeks in my life. Intense basic training with live ammo was the order of the day—run by cadre who had just returned from the midwinter battle of Inchon Reservoir. Minus ears, toes, teeth, arms, and what have you, these teachers of death were mean clear through, having tasted the bitter experience of war at a very young and impressionable age. Their sole objective in life at that moment in time was to prepare us recruits to cope with the same experience they had suffered through, with as much success as possible.

And they certainly had the backing of management, which thoroughly endorsed the principle of tough preparation. The training company immediately preceding us learned that the hard way. In the seventeenth week, training culminated in a full-scale offensive with live ammunition, flame throwers, mortars, field artillery, and air force bombing. Normally, it was carefully orchestrated to avoid injury and death among participants. Not so with our ill-fated brethren—officers approved proceeding with the attack in a drenching rainstorm. The rain dampened the firing increments in the mortars, which dictated how far the shells transversed. The shells fell short among the troops and instructors, leaving several dead, wounded, or crazed. Fortunately, the weather was perfect a week or two later, when our company went through the same exercise.

At last our training was over, and I was looking for the thirty-six pounds I had lost. Our final act was a formation ceremony in front of company headquarters. One hundred-seventy strong were we, lined up to receive our assignments.

Pressure mounted as the company clerk intoned name after name designated for the front lines of Korea. He finally came to mine, announcing "Martin, CIC School in Fort Holabird, Maryland." What a relief. Only one other individual was designated for further training.

The remaining 168 were immediately shipped to Korea to man foxholes on the edge of death. Just two days later, two-thirds of our graduated company were killed in a midnight enemy attack.

By the grace of God, I had been spared for another time. Never has my name sounded so good as it did on that grim day of choice in 1951.

❧ The Whitman Massacre

A time and place for everything—
Ah, to know just when or where.
Such insight surely for us would bring
A life secure from what's out there.

August 1, 1966, was a blistering-hot day in Austin, Texas, with the temperature destined to peak well over 100 degrees by late afternoon. It started out to be one of those lazy mid-summer Mondays that even experienced Texans find hard to take, with nothing moving that didn't have to, including the wind.

In the face of this, my inveterate squash partner and I drove onto the University of Texas campus at 11:40 A.M., our usual arrival time, for a noontime match in Gregory Gym. As we approached the gym, we noticed two vacant parking spaces. We needed change to feed the meter, so we chose the space that was farther away from the gym entrance, because it was in the shade and would allow us more comfortable waiting for a pedestrian with pocket change.

As we waited momentarily for change, we heard what we thought was a car backfiring somewhere nearby. Thinking nothing of it, we negotiated our needed change with a passerby, fed the meter, and entered the gym. The squash courts were located in the basement of the stoutly built building; therefore, we were impervious to what might be going on around us as we pursued a squash match with our usual competitive fervor.

It was not until after the match that we learned with horror from an agitated conversation among others in the gym's steamroom what was going on outside the building. Less than two blocks away, Charles Whitman was waging a one-man war against UT students and Austin citizens from his vantage point on top of the high-rise tower of the UT administration building! Armed with multiple weapons and plentiful ammunition, Whitman was in the process of killing sixteen people and injuring thirty-one others.

In a state of shock and disbelief, we showered and dressed and gingerly left the building through an exit away from the tower. Keeping the gym between us and Whitman, we witnessed what was going on in our area of the campus. It was an incredible scene of temporary anarchy in full sway. Running every which way were seemingly leaderless, armed individuals using buildings and trees for temporary cover while firing potshots at the tower. Policemen, UT security guards, firemen, and individuals who had raced home to add their deer rifles to the mayhem all searched diligently for a one-way look at the tower.

While all this firepower was not endangering Whitman, who was hiding on a walkway behind a stout balustrade that circled the tower near its summit, it was serving a purpose. Whitman could no longer lean over the railing and easily pick off more victims. He had to remain essentially in a defensive posture by the time we left Gregory Gym. Wrap-up time was near, and it was not long before heroic efforts by two Austin policemen and a deputized veteran provided closure to perhaps the most hideous incident in the history of Texas' capital city. Whitman was killed on the tower walkway, and it was over.

During the next twenty-four hours or so, my squash partner and I learned that Whitman had succeeded in killing one person across the street from Gregory Gym and two more a few hundred yards beyond the gym. We also learned that Whitman started his firing from the tower at 11:40 A.M., aiming first at the Gregory Gym sector of the campus in his deadly walk around the tower summit.

Then a startling thought occurred to both of us at the same instant. We already knew that the parking space we had selected the day before in the shade was safely situated under the protective wing of Gregory Gym. But what about the space in the sunlight and closer to the gym that we had shunned? We raced out to the campus to park in that "shunned" space, which was once again empty. We climbed out of the car and stood by the parking meter. We looked up and were aghast. At 11:40 A.M. the previous day, we would have been waiting motionless for two minutes seeking parking meter change in full view of the UT tower!

❧ Premonition at Work

**No one wants to be on the next page
Of a life that's suddenly gone ...**

It was a beautiful morning in Austin, Texas, on November 22, 1963. There was a touch of excitement in the air as the city waited in eager anticipation for the arrival of President John F. Kennedy and his First Lady, "Jackie," later that afternoon. Vice President Lyndon B. Johnson, along with Lady Bird and other Texas dignitaries, would add to the prominence of the occasion.

While my wife and I could not attend the banquet to be held in the president's honor at Palmer Auditorium in the downtown area that evening, there was a special event in store for me, at least. My ninth-floor office looked out over the projected parade route that the president would take on the way to the auditorium. There was an added plus. The office building was old-fashioned, and I could throw open my window to enjoy both the sight and sound of the festive parade.

My employer had recently moved from another building, and our offices were still not completely settled. There were materials at home, including a long T-square, a yardstick, and other items of similar length that I wanted in the office. I chose that morning to bring them in, wrapped in newspaper for easy handling.

Arriving at about 8:30 A.M., I stopped in the coffee shop on the first floor for an eye opener. When I propped my package against the counter, the shop manager asked what it was. I told her and then said: "Come to think of it, this package almost looks like a rifle wrapped in camouflage. Since we are on the president's parade route today, I'm surprised there aren't any Secret Service agents around checking on things like this." As I left for my office, we agreed there was probably too much parade territory to cover to expect agents to interview people in our building, particularly since most of the available agents were probably busy in Fort Worth and Dallas covering the planned presidential activity in that area.

When I reached my office, I immediately went to my window, opened it, and leaned out to look at the parade route half expecting someone to question what I was doing. It was with a weird feeling that I turned back to my desk, fervently hoping that no one in Texas would use a open high-rise window to fire upon the president that day.

Three hours later, my hope was shattered when Lee Harvey Oswald did just that in Dallas, with devastating results.

☜ Life and Death Are Not Always What They Seem

When you cast illusion
You create confusion.
What is never was
And therefore will cause
A most erroneous conclusion!

Many individuals approaching so-called middle age tend to view their fortieth birthday as a millstone in lieu of the milestone it should be. My wife and I were no exception to the rule and approached the created crisis together; I say together, because as I mentioned previously, we are virtually the same age in years and days, if not hours and minutes. To combat the growing dread, we decided, or at least I decided, to make light of it in a somewhat questionable but unforgettable way. By happenstance, we, along with our two preteen daughters, were visiting my brother and his family in Barre, Vermont, the "Granite Center of the World," where the famous Rock of Ages firm supplies much of the nation with polished tombstones. What better place to stage a mock funeral in honor of our completing four decades.

Utilizing my ministerial father's connections with a prominent funeral director in town, I tried to commandeer a hearse for the occasion. Looking back on this pageant, I have thanked my lucky stars that it was not available on the desired day, for it undoubtedly would have pushed matters over the edge. It was tough enough keeping all participants harnessed without that emblem of finality heading our parade. Nevertheless, the director did the next best thing by providing us with car fender flags that are typically used in funeral processions, at least in the northern states.

Appropriate black bunting was utilized, along with a black banner decrying the age forty, to dress up the cars in the procession. We used three cars to transport my wife and me and our daughters, along with my brother and his wife and their three preteen children, from the downtown Methodist church to the Hope Cemetery, located on the town's outskirts. Fender flags, along with turned-on headlights, attracted the desired attention (or undesired by all the other family members) of local citizens fortunate enough to witness the solemn parade. I even spotted a doffed hat or two as we moved slowly through Barre's streets!

When we reached the cemetery, our daughters, nephew, and two nieces came unglued. To put it charitably, they thought we had lost our minds. Our graveside ceremony to end the event was met with rolled eyes and groans of embarrassment, and the sense of reverence over the solemn occasion was totally lost. So we closed it down with picture-taking and a sense of well-being that promised things would soon get better.

And they did! After the graveside ceremony, I took one of the cars to go downtown to make a quick purchase at a pharmacy. I parked out front and decided not to feed the meter, since I would only be there a moment. The gods were not yet beginning to smile, however, for the chief of police came by and began writing a ticket while I was in the store. When I came out and saw what he was doing, I rushed up to him and said, "Surely, officer, you're not going to give me a parking ticket after all I've been through today" and pointed to the front of my car. At that, he looked up and, seeing the fender flags for the first time, exclaimed, "I'm so sorry." He promptly tore up the ticket, bowed his head, and moved on.

❧ Meditations From the Heart Skip a Beat

The tie that binds is no tenuous thread;
It is a rope as strong as steel.
Family gifts through generations tread
Stirring hidden bonds that seal.

My mother was a complex person. On the one side, she was quite English—an intelligent, practical, heritage-oriented, and economically driven individual. On the other, she was a very religious, warm, and humorous person involved in the arts. She was an accomplished musician, for example, who patiently instilled a deep love for music into my being.

However, I was a normal boy who preferred football and baseball over piano lessons. Nevertheless, I gradually came to know and love good music. Mother would carefully tune in the opera every Saturday afternoon through a distant New York City radio station. We also attended concerts; she maneuvered an usher position for me so that I could attend for free while providing my parents with gratis box seats. I became acquainted with such artists as Rubenstein and Serkin playing the greatest piano concertos of all time.

Mother, who played in the State Symphony Orchestra, practiced on her violin at home. Her favorite piece was "Meditations From Thaïs." Well, all this parental influence finally took hold on me, and I played in six bands, married into a musical family, sang in several church choirs with my wife, served on symphony boards, and provided our children ample opportunity to know and appreciate good music.

While, for one reason or another, our two daughters did not take an active role in music, they were certainly made aware of the value of the musical world. In fact, they welcomed music as part of their experience.

This paid off when our granddaughter came along and evidenced real musical talent. Dawn became a member of one of Texas' leading high school symphonic bands, playing an excellent clarinet. When asked to strengthen another section of the band, she ended up playing a fine trombone as well.

In one of her marching band contests, the band played the last movement of Tschaikovsky's Fourth Symphony, bringing tears to my eyes. It was my Mother's favorite symphony. A few months later, Dawn was participating in a state district contest with her solo clarinet. She was allowed to choose her own piece to play.

I did not know what she had chosen when I asked her to play for me in a private rendition. She began to play, and I could not believe my ears. I was listening to the haunting strains of "Meditations From Thaïs!"

☙ **What God Hath Wrought**

The fifth dimension is really quite neat;
It can scare Tom and Harry and even old Pete.
    But when logic prevails,
    It disperses tall tales
And truth leaps out from behind that white sheet!

It was August 23, a hot and somewhat hopeless day.
My car was in the shop, along with my garage door
opener, which I had failed to retrieve and bring home.
This oversight led me to park my strange-looking rental
car along the curb in front of my house instead of in
our garage. Late that night, thanks to some mother's ghastly child,
its rear window was shattered like a University of Texas Longhorn's
Alliance Bowl dream.

Early the next morning, an already-tired meter reader—overwhelmed
with the unpopular nature of his job, which lays the predicate for
incredible August utility bills—rang our doorbell. Eager to please
someone at long last, Mr. Goodwrench breathlessly advised my wife
that someone had violated our vehicle. My wife looked out at the
street and in a relieved voice advised him it was not our car.

Not content to let matters rest, Mr. G., still searching for ways to
improve his image, immediately woke up the neighbors across the
street to let them know the damaged vehicle was not ours. "Was it
theirs?" he asked. Following their unhappy *no*, he left more unpopular than ever.

After my wife's alert, I rushed out to survey the damage. The first
thing I noticed was our neighbor standing on her front porch talking
into her portable phone. She was saying: "No, Officer, we don't own
the car, and our neighbors across the street don't either; we think it
is probably stolen."

I called 911 to report the vandalism and to straighten the mess out.
The officer responded, "Are you reporting a stolen vehicle?" I closed

my eyes, bit my lip, and held the tears in, for I knew I had a long morning in front of me.

One week later, on yet another desultory August morn, chapter two of this incredible saga unfolded before me. I was rushing out to administer the latest garbage-sorting requirements of the city, when an indescribable crashing sound filled my ears. I looked around and saw nothing. The street was empty, and deathly stillness filled the air. With visions of the fifth dimension filling my mind, I rushed out to the street and finally saw it—the rear end of a car that had wedged through two trees along our lot line, demolishing our border fence. It was now hanging precariously across our dry creek chasm.

There was no one in the car!

Neighbors began to converge, all asking where the car came from and how many were hurt. Requests to call 911 were legion. They were unnecessary, for as I looked across the street, the neighbor who lives next door to the "stolen car" neighbor was busy talking to the police on her portable phone.

I heard her say, "Officer, someone has crashed their car into the woods across the street from our house. Is there anyone hurt? I don't know— let me run down and look. (Their house is on a steep incline.) Oh my God, that's *my* car; so no, there's no one in it. But how did it get there?"

This is hard to believe. The lady had driven her car up her steep driveway, rounding a partial curve to enter her garage. She parked the car, left it, pressed the switch to close her garage door, and went into the house. She then heard a loud noise and rushed out the front door to see what was the matter. Thinking her own car was safely in the closed garage, she got her portable phone to report the "accident" across the street.

It took a neighborhood discussion to piece the puzzle together. Somehow, our neighbor had left her car in her garage in neutral without using the brakes. The car began its roll in time to slip out of the garage before the automatic garage door trapped it inside. The rest is history.

Unusual things come in threes, and I was convinced this portable phone saga had not yet reached its end. Sure enough, it was hardly more than a week later when my wife and the lady next door, both of whom live across the street from the "stolen car" lady and the "car accident" lady, completed destiny.

The lady next door had recently given birth to her first baby, so my wife prepared a meal for her and her family and asked me to deliver it— the meal, that is. As I was laying the meal out in the kitchen, the lady's phone began to ring in a persistent manner. I finally suggested that she needed to answer it and that I would let myself out.

I was about to enter our own home when my wife burst out of the door breathlessly, noting that the governor was on the portable phone she was carrying. So there I am on the front lawn at 5 P.M. trying to talk with the governor of Texas as the endless parade of early-evening planes began flying over our home in the flight path that the real estate agent who sold our lot to us failed to mention back in 1962.

Later I learned that when the governor first called, my wife gave her the number of our neighbor, because I was there delivering food. It was the governor making the phone ring when I suggested I would let myself out, thus leaving the "new baby" neighbor with an undoubtedly unique experience to share with her baby at a later date.

The moral of this neighborhood tale is simply this: If you must use your portable phone outside in the yard, beware of the consequences.

⋈ In the Eye of a Turkicane

> **Have you ever told a story no one will believe**
> **With a wink of their eye and a laugh up their sleeve,**
> **Saying your pull of the wool**
> **Is for the eyes of a fool?**
> **Then read this true tale before I take leave.**

Have you ever been in the eye of a hurricane? It is an experience you will never forget. It has happened to me twice. The first time occurred when I was a lad of nine; my family and I found ourselves in the path of the infamous hurricane of 1938 that roared through New England before dissipating in Quebec, Canada. This was back in the days before the authorities gave names to hurricanes and spent days warning the public of their advance. Thus, we did not expect the organized mayhem a big hurricane provides, particularly since we were more than 200 miles inland from the Atlantic. Only big, fast-moving hurricanes can travel that far over land without the eye of the storm disintegrating.

Virtually the same thing happened to us in Austin, Texas, twenty-three years later, when Hurricane Carla flew over Austin before disintegrating some thirty-five miles farther north over Taylor, Texas. Again, the eye provided an awesome experience. The atmosphere was absolutely calm, the stars and moon appeared, and there was no hint of the remaining half of the hurricane poised to attack our feeling of tranquillity. Bottom line, the experience was very similar to the first one in 1938, despite storm naming, presumed progress in the field of meteorology and improved communications giving ample warning.

But this story is not about the eyes of hurricanes. As fascinating as it is to experience them, I have found several people who have shared that experience. In fact, TV coverage will provide you with that experience ad nauseum during every hurricane season. No, this is about an eye, a deceiving, peaceful eye that I have experienced and have yet to find anyone else who has!

This incredible story begins and ends in the early 1970s on a large ranch in the Texas Hill Country southwest of Kerrville, widely claimed to be God's country by true believers in the know. I was among privileged guests of a magnanimous host, who invited us annually for a pampered weekend of deer hunting and skeet shooting. The ranch foreman was a Texas A&M graduate who really knew his stuff when it came to analyzing the wild and its inhabitants. I had mildly impressed him over the years with my penchant for finding wild turkey, since they were few and far between on the ranch. I hasten to add it was not skill, but rather an indescribable something I have yet to harness for anything worthwhile.

One afternoon, the foreman was driving me out to my favorite deer blind, responding to my endless nature-related questions with lengthy dissertation. As he was talking, I looked off to the left and spotted a large flock of turkeys—at least thirty Thanksgiving dinners' worth—walking single file through a grove of live oak and brush some 125 yards away. Pleased that I had seen this phenomenon first, I alerted the foreman, who almost lost his cool. He recovered in time to move his jeep forward to a place where I could disembark and take aim at a gobbler.

Since I had only a .30-06 rifle handy, I aimed at the very top of the back of the selected bird, for the simple reason that a lower shot would have resulted in total disintegration. (For those who may not know, a shotgun is the weapon of choice in turkey and bird hunting). I fired, and—despite the loud report of my weapon—absolutely nothing happened! It was as though I had fired at the sun in the opposite direction with a silencer. The entire flock of turkeys continued to walk slowly forward, and my selected target appeared unscathed.

This does not happen in real life, Dear Reader. At the least unnatural sound, wild turkey take off faster than a Concorde. What was going on? I aimed at another bird and fired. Same result! While I felt my marksman medals in service should have brought this story to immediate conclusion, I let the foreman try his professional hand. He did no better!

While he was performing futilely, I looked around for an answer to the puzzle and found it. There were two hawks circling in the sky over the turkey flock. The turkey were more scared of their natural enemy than they were of us; thus their reluctance to take off in normal fashion. The hawks also provided the answer to our "faulty" marksmanship. Frightened turkey raise the feathers on their back about two inches. Sure enough; when we walked over to the path taken by the turkeys, we found three clumps of feathers about two inches long, which restored our faith in our attained marksmanship, but did nothing for our Thanksgiving dinner scheduled for the following week.

The foreman drove me on to my lease station, which was only one-half mile beyond the site of the turkey incident. In fact, I had followed the progress of the turkeys after the shooting and noticed they climbed the hill adjacent to my blind. However, when I climbed into my blind there was no evidence of turkey anywhere, and I quickly reverted to a deer-hunting mode.

It was a warm afternoon, and nothing was moving. I was on the verge of napping, when I spotted the two hawks seen earlier, circling the top of the adjacent hill some four hundred yards away. Curiosity got the better of me, and I made the calculated decision to climb the substantial hill with my cumbersome and heavy gear. As I made my sweaty ascent, I noted that the top of the hill was covered by forest, brush, and large rocks. The hawks remained the only moving creatures besides me until I spooked a deer about twenty-five yards from the top of the hill.

An inner call of destiny restrained me from pursuing the deer. Such prey could come later. As I approached the rocky summit of the hill, absolute silence reigned. Not a leaf stirred, not a sound occurred. I felt like I was entering a natural tomb as I passed the first ring of trees into a dark, stealthy stillness. I moved forward another ten yards or so to the very center of the hilltop and experienced an eerie sensation. Somehow, I didn't belong there!

And then it happened! All hell broke loose—with a huge whirring sound, the members of the turkey flock took off running in a circle around me and out the other side of the mountain top. In less than ten seconds, the eye of the turkicane had disintegrated, leaving me stunned, with weapon frozen in midair. Somehow, I had breached the flock's circle of defense without spotting a feather or a movement of any kind, only to be left alone finally in charge of the hill.

In honor of this one-of-a-kind experience provided me by the wild turkey flock, I left the glen and fired at the hawks, allowing the flock to fly off to freedom, so richly deserved. Needless to say, this experience ended my turkey-hunting career, for when you achieve the ultimate there is nothing left to do but move on!

epilogue

And so I have—moved on, that is, and will come to the inevitable conclusion that may someday grace my tombstone, or better yet, the roadside that leads to it:

> **Thanks to Lois, his lovely wife,**
> **And the many others in his life;**
> **He never had a lonely thought**
> **About the farm he finally bought!**

Buy Burma Shave.

Julian G. Martin and his family have lived in Austin, Texas, for almost a half-century. He experienced multiple careers in counterintelligence, governmental research, and the energy industry and has written numerous articles and research documents for publication. In the early 1990s, he was a key resource person and editor for the book entitled *Texas Oil, American Dreams*, a history of independent oilmen in Texas authored by nationally renowned Dr. Larry Goodwyn of Duke University.

In retirement, Julian has chosen to spend much of his time reading and writing, tutoring students, conducting student and VIP tours at the LBJ Library in Austin, performing church work, conducting mediation and role modeling, working with seniors through board programs with the New Life Institute and the Austin Community College, relating to family, and traveling. He plays duplicate bridge, golf, and squash on a regular basis and conducts seminars on limericks for relaxation. He is a member of the board of trustees for the Southwest Research Institute in San Antonio, an appointed delegate to Interstate Oil and Gas Compact Commission, and a member of the Foundation for Religious Studies in Texas. In 1996 he was selected Man of the Year by the Texas Independent Producers and Royalty Owners Association.